passion.

driven.

profession.

denise conway

Suite 300 - 990 Fort St
Victoria, BC, Canada, V8V 3K2
www.friesenpress.com

Copyright © 2016 by Denise Conway
First Edition — 2016

All rights reserved.

No part of this publication may be reproduced in any form, or by any means, electronic or mechanical, including photocopying, recording, or any information browsing, storage, or retrieval system, without permission in writing from FriesenPress.

ISBN
978-1-4602-3087-9 (Hardcover)
978-1-4602-3088-6 (Paperback)
978-1-4602-3089-3 (eBook)

1. Business & Economics, Careers, Job Hunting

Distributed to the trade by The Ingram Book Company

TABLE OF CONTENTS

chapter 1   1
    The Employability Assessment Model?

chapter 2   9
    Do I Have Clear Career Goals?

chapter 3   47
    Will The Labour Market Support My Choice?

chapter 4   53
    Do I Have The Skills And Requirements?

chapter 5   73
    Empowering Beliefs?

chapter 6   89
    Do I Know How And Where To Look For Work? Am I Able To Maintain A Job?

chapter 7   101
    Goal Setting?

INTRODUCTION

Picture yourself waking up every morning excited about going to work. You're fascinated that you actually get paid to do something you love so much. Sadly, this is just a dream for most. Fact is, statistics show that close to eighty percent of people in the workforce are unsatisfied with their present jobs. Over the last decades the world has seen dramatic changes that have greatly affected the labour force.

Economic swings have led to restructuring, down-sizing, bankruptcies…long gone are the days where a person spent the majority of his or her life in the same job, retiring with a nice gold watch and a pension. Today it is common for the average person to experience nine to twelve different occupations between graduating and making it to retirement. Passion Driven Profession addresses this reality with a positive and proven approach for change.

Given the fact that we spend sixty percent of our time working, it shouldn't and doesn't have to be painful. Instead, you can find something you love to do and then find a way to get paid for it. You may be asking the question, "So what makes you such an authority on the topic?" A fair query to be sure. While I will be going into specific detail throughout the book, let me take this time to give you a brief background on myself and on why I wrote this book.

My passion is helping people. From when I was a little girl I would always go out of my way to help others. Anytime anyone asked what I wanted to be when I grew up, I would respond "I want to be a teacher." Making a difference in people's lives has always been an important aspect of who I feel I was created to be. I like to believe the best about everyone. For the past twenty years I have been involved in career counselling; guiding people who are looking for the right occupational path. Along the way I have accumulated much knowledge from various sources, including education, experience, respected experts, and clients I have taught. Add to that my own personal history of searching for that dream job while raising children as a single mom. With this background, I am confident that what I have to offer can truly be life altering.

It is my belief that it is difficult to know what profession we are meant to follow until we take the time to 'soul search' and understand ourselves better. The following pages will introduce information and exercises that will challenge you to become more self-aware and show how to apply this to your search for that perfect job fit. We will examine questions that will assist you in determining your path, as well as other important and related issues such as coping with change, and how to assess the labour market and the opportunities available. Of course, because I do not profess to be the 'know all and end all' of the subject, the book also offers other valuable resources such as web sites and information on organizations that can be instrumental to your success.

Remember the bottom line…you DON'T have to settle for any old job just to get a paycheque. In fact, you'll discover that a profession can be about so much more than simply making a living. With direction, perseverance, and the right insight, you can finally find the job of your dreams.

Find the work that you love and you will never work a day in your life.

Enjoy the journey!

chapter 1

THE EMPLOYABILITY ASSESSMENT MODEL?

Five Crucial Questions You Need to Explore

An old Chinese proverb says, "You can give a man a fish and feed him for a day, but TEACH him to fish and you can feed him for a lifetime." Many individuals have been floundering throughout their occupational lives because they just don't know what they truly should be considering when deciding on the right career.

There is so much more to discovering your dream job than simply having a nice resume, knocking on doors, or enrolling in an educational program. I have found through my years of experience in career counselling that if people are taught a comprehensive and well thought-out approach to job searching, their chances for success are considerably increased; in essence, teaching them to be their own career counsellors.

In this opening chapter I will give you an overall view of five questions that I consider extremely important in ascertaining the correct path in your pursuit of the right career. Subsequent chapters will explore each individual question in more detail. It is important to note also that the questions should be explored in their exact order. If you can't identify and clearly answer question #1, there is no reason to even bother looking at any of the other questions. You are not ready to move on until that question is explored and satisfied. The Five Questions are as follows:

1. Do I have clear career goals?
2. Will the labour market support my choice?
3. Do I have the skills and requirements?
4. Do I know how and where to look for work?
5. Am I able to maintain a job?

I was first introduced to the service-needs assessment, or employability model as it is also known, in the early 1990s when I started at Human Resources Development Canada (HRDC). This department of the government was a pioneer in employment counselling at a time when there was only one course in the country. It was also a time of major recession and industries were falling.

Prior to this period, HRDC would see seasonal employees such as construction workers and teachers, or people who had been in high turn-over jobs such as hairdressing or the service industry. Now, however, with the world as we knew it on the brink of globalization and major change, suddenly we at HRDC were seeing everyone from engineers to persons in high-tech occupations.

The area I worked in at the time, the Niagara region, had the second highest unemployment rate in the country. In the beginning, my role was to assess unemployed clients for employment counsellors. One on one counselling soon became non-existent, however, and eventually I was trained for group counselling; the philosophy being that under those circumstances, we could see a lot more people in a short amount of time. Originally, the groups were segregated: unemployment insurance claimants in one group and social service clients in another. But it soon became apparent that everyone in a jobless situation has the same needs and that's how this assessment model came to be.

Question 1 – Do I Have Clear Career Goals?

This is probably the most important question you need to ask yourself, which is why it is the lead-off question. If you haven't determined what your goals are, there is really no sense in moving forward to the subsequent questions. Chapter 2 will explore this question in much greater depth and will challenge you to identify your personality type as well as your values and interests. It will also help you assess other important factors relating to your career goals such as; requirements (skills and education); the prospects available in that field and in particular geographical areas; work hours; physical capabilities; and environmental conditions.

Question 2 – Will the Labour Market Support My Choice?

Once you have identified your career goals, it is important to research the availability of positions related to your choice. The chapter dedicated to this question will give you insight into how and where to access Labour Market information, including web sites and other useful resources such as newspapers, libraries, and government programs.

Question 3 – Do I Have the Skills and Job Requirements?

This question is about much more than just experience, or education and training that may be required to enter a certain occupation. It also includes assessment of other factors such as licences, trade tickets, and special equipment and tools that you may need to have for a specific job, as well as the costs you will have to consider.

Question 4 – Do I Know How and Where to Look for Work?

This section deals with more traditional topics in employment exploration, such as cover letters, resume writing, and interview techniques. It will also give you a better idea of how to go about searching for employment effectively; such as Internet job searching, networking, and the importance of thoroughly researching organizations and companies in which you may be interested in seeking employment.

Question 5 – Am I Able to Maintain a Job?

Once you have addressed and assessed each of the previous questions, you will have to consider whether you have any issues that may prevent you from maintaining a job once you are hired. Many people may meet educational requirements and have plenty of related experience in certain occupations, but that does not guarantee career longevity if there are factors in their lives that can cause complications in their employment.

Poor work habits, conflicts with co-workers and/or supervisors, and transportation issues must be taken into consideration. The presence of any addictions is of course another issue that can be a major hindrance and should be dealt with before an individual seriously begins considering his or her future.

We will consider possible 'road blocks' that may be encountered and how to deal with them in order to ensure your best possibility for success. Throughout this journey I will continually remind you and encourage you to get into the habit of actually writing things down. This will bring the journey you are about to embark on more 'into picture' and give it a little more substance. You will find it helpful if you do the exercises and keep records concerning the details of your goals, such as target dates for attaining them and where you hope to be in so many years down the road.

This model, when appropriately grasped, will prevent you from walking into five different places in search of help and walking out more confused than when you went in. It will help you open your eyes to a better way of looking for work. Some people become desperate to the point of accepting any kind of employment; but will that get them to where they would really like to be?

Before we move on, I would like to share with you an interesting *Atlantic Journal* article that I came across: "The world is too big for us.

Too much going on, too many crimes, too much violence and excitement. Try as you will, you get behind in the race, in spite of yourself. It's an incessant strain to keep pace...and still, you lose ground. Science empties its discoveries on you so fast that you stagger beneath them in hopeless bewilderment. The political world is news seen so rapidly you're out of breath trying to keep pace with who's in and who's out. Everything is high pressure. Human nature can't endure much more!"

Now try and guess when this article was written. You may be very surprised at the date. This was written in the early 1900s following the market crash of 1910 and the end of World War I. It was a time when the earth's population was 1.75 billion. Homes were now being supplied with electricity, which had led to such inventions as the refrigerator, the washing machine, and the vacuum cleaner. Manned flight was in its infancy and the existence of the telephone was revolutionizing the way people communicated. The medical world had advanced with the invention of the X-ray.

Now we live in a time where cell phones are commonplace and we have been connected to the rest of the world and its available information via the Internet. People fly daily to any destination they want, including space if you have the kind of money it takes to be a space tourist. The world's population now tops over six and a half billion and is projected to reach well over eight billion in the next fifteen years.

I mention these facts to give us a better perspective on just what kind of crazy, stress-filled, and fast-paced world we now live in. The aforementioned *Atlantic Journal* article could very well have been written today. Advancements in technology have changed the face of employment and have actually eliminated many jobs in some cases. I find it hard to keep up with this ever-changing technology.

Some people find themselves lost in limbo when the only job they've known for thirty-some years is suddenly taken away from them and they are forced to start over. For those people I contend: When a door closes on you it is time to look for that open window of opportunity. Just as technological progress has eliminated some jobs, it has also opened new opportunities in the employment world. You may be one of those people who find themselves 'back at the drawing board' or someone just starting out in the world of work and wondering what it is you would like to do and should be doing. Be assured – the possibilities and opportunities are out there; you just have to know how and where to find them.

We all go through tough times and we all carry a certain amount of 'baggage' with us, but there is always help available if you really want it and there is always hope. I can personally attest to this and want to share my experiences and knowledge with all those who find themselves coping with an uncertain and unstable employment situation.

If you pay close attention to the Five Questions, I am sure that you will be pleased with the end results and will finally find yourself working in an occupation that brings you fulfillment and satisfaction. You will even get to know yourself better and will adopt a more positive attitude, not only regarding work but your life in general.

A Glimpse into My Own Work History

It took me quite some time and several job moves before I came this point in my life; working in an occupation that brings me so much joy and allows me to flourish. Throughout the book I will be expanding on the various occupations I've held, but for now I would like to give you a brief overview. Perhaps many of you will be able to identify with my personal history.

As young people, many of us are introduced to the labour force through simple jobs that give us the opportunity to make a little money, supplementing the weekly allowance our parents might have been kind enough to allot us. For some it might come in the form of a paper route or shovelling the neighbours' driveways. For me, it was working on a fruit farm picking strawberries. Eventually, I went on to work as a clerk in a local drug store. I realized at one point that I would have to further my education for a chance to find the right job. When I couldn't get into a course for my original choice, I decided to take a shot at being a bilingual secretary. But I soon discovered that this was not the occupation for me.

Later on, I was able to enrol in and graduate from an Early Childhood Education course. After this, I not only spent time as an educator of young children, but I also tried my hand at operating my own daycare. However, my circumstances at the time caused me to seek out a better-paying job, which ultimately brought me to the wonderful world of career counselling; an occupation I have been involved in for well over twenty years. But even this career wasn't without its curves in the road.

I went from working directly for HRDC, to a job that was contracted out by the government when they opened up the first employment service provider centre, St. Leonard's Society of Brant. But when I was hired by a big corporate trainer in Mississauga, I was given a better opportunity, and this is where I really honed my skills in the field of corporate training.

As much as I enjoyed this job, two years of the daily commute made for a long day away from home, and I didn't see much of my children during this period. So eventually, I opened my own company, Training Trends, teaching counsellors from all over Ontario. The company flourished for a while until two major events that would change my situation; 9/11, and the effect it had on the world; and a difficult relationship with which I had become caught up, and the effect it had on my life and work.

It became very difficult to continue having a positive influence on my clients when my home life was in disarray. I needed to get away from everything my life was at that time so I moved away from career counselling all together and took employment as a customer service representative, with Fallsview Casino in Niagara Falls.

I persevered in that position for three years but was unaccustomed to the hours and shifts required of me. Consequently, once again, I decided to return to my roots and attempted to open my own counselling business; Career Quest. However, the endeavour was made difficult by my circumstances at the time, and I was forced to abandon the project.

Fortunately, I was able to secure employment with another employment counselling group, a third-party organization contracted by Service Ontario (formerly HRDC), and that's where I am at the present. When you speak to other people, you will often find similar stories. There are even some who have experienced more employment changes than I did.

My goal of producing a book related to my career actually originated several years ago. Success does not come overnight. It involves perseverance, hard work, and a true desire to realize a dream. Study this book carefully and start making plans to achieve the goals that will change your life!

chapter 2

DO I HAVE CLEAR CAREER GOALS?

Learning Who You Really Are and What You Really Need and Want

> *"Without goals and plans to reach them, you are like a ship that has set sail with no destination."*
>
> Fitzhugh Dodson, clinical psychologist, author, and child-rearing expert.

So many people are unhappy with their employment situations and have experienced a lifetime of job-jumping, because they have failed to identify specific goals they hope to achieve. However, just recognizing these goals is not enough and will not guarantee success. A plan to follow in pursuit of them must first be developed and implemented. That is why it is so important to explore this first question in the employability assessment model. There are many factors and questions to consider when deciding on your career goals.

When exploring what kind of work you are looking for, you will need to address the following criteria:

1) *What type of money do I need or want?* Today's society has placed a lot of importance on money and although it doesn't guarantee that you'll be happy with your occupation, everyone needs a certain wage to survive. What kind of lifestyle do you want? How much do you need? In 1985, I graduated from Early Childhood Education and became director of a daycare. At the time, the position paid $16,900. That may sound okay, but I happened to be a single mother who was struggling to pay the bills so it was not sufficient for my needs. I was motivated to seek other employment and this led me to a government job as a career counsellor.

2) *What is my situation regarding work hours?* Certain occupations require specific hours of work. For example, someone in the manufacturing trade might expect to work three different shifts, while someone in the service industry will likely have to work a lot of afternoons as well as weekends. You have to figure out whether your work schedule will be conducive to your situation. For instance, if you have children you must ascertain how your schedule will affect them.

3) *Do I have transportation issues?* When looking at career possibilities, you must take into consideration how you will get to work. Do you have a reliable vehicle or will you need to rely on public transit? Will you have to actually relocate to accommodate your choice, and is that feasible for you?

4) *What limitations might I have?* It is also important to consider any factors such as disabilities you may have. For example, if you suffer from back problems, you wouldn't do very well in an occupation where heavy lifting is required.

5) *Do I have the proper support system in place that is beneficial to my career goals?* When I was attempting to open my own career-counselling business, Career Quest, I happened to be going through a very trying time, with health issues and a recent marital separation. At that point in my life I had little to no support system, which simply was not conducive to me reaching my goals. Thankfully, my health problems all worked out fine and I landed on my feet. There is always hope!

6) *What type of experience and education is required of me?* Many employers will be looking for a certain amount of experience for a position they are seeking to fill. If you are lacking in this department, you might consider looking into a volunteer job that is related to the position, to gain more experience and see if it is something you'd really like to do.

Education has always been an important component when it comes to searching for a career. A high school diploma isn't enough anymore. What kind of advanced learning will you need, and are you in a financial position to pursue that degree? You are well aware that if your dream job is to become a doctor, you will have to spend many years in school, not to mention that it will cost a considerable amount of money. If this is not plausible in your present situation, you may want to look at a related field, such as nursing or paramedics. You might discover that this may suffice or that you can use these jobs as stepping stones towards your ultimate goal when you are in a better position to do so. This brings up another important question:

7) *Are my goals short-term or long-term?* What kind of steps or stages have you established in your plan and what kind of time-line are you looking at?

8) *What type of work am I interested in?* This is probably the most important question you can ask yourself when deciding on career goals. Obviously, you will not do well in a school program or an occupation if your interests are not met and your motivation is therefore hindered. Many people set themselves up for failure when they make the wrong choices in the beginning or along the way. We will explore decision-making in greater detail in a later chapter but in the meantime, we need to look at ourselves more deeply and what it is that constitutes and influences our interests.

How Well Do You Really Know Yourself?

"Man's Pygmalion project has been to make all those around him just like him. Fortunately, this is impossible. To sculpt the other into his own likeness fails before it begins...remove the fangs of the lion and, behold, a toothless lion, not a domestic cat. Attempts to change the spouse, offspring, or a student or employee can create change, but the result is a scar, not a transformation."

These words of renowned psychologist David Keirsey remind us just how unique each of us is. Science recognizes that personality actually begins to form in the womb about sixteen weeks into gestation. While our personalities may continue to be influenced and shaped by many environmental factors while we are young, their basic foundation has already been established by the time we are born.

The Bible even makes reference to the fact, saying, "God knew us in our mother's womb before we were born" (Jeremiah 1:15). It is my personal belief that God created us for a specific purpose in life, loves us enough to want us to succeed, and has equipped us with the skills to do so. The Scriptures also state; "God is no respecter of persons" (Acts 10:34). In other words, what He does for one person, He will do for another. No one is exempt from His goodness and guidance.

Now you may not be a believer and it is not my intention to attempt to convert anyone religiously; I just feel it necessary to mention that I believe my success has been largely in part because of the gifts He has blessed me with, and because of how I have come to recognize these gifts. I thank Him daily for this. God has given each of us our own special skills and gifts to deal with and succeed in life.

I've been told that when I was younger, I was an incessant talker. Apparently, I just never shut up, I wasn't even able to stop talking during church service and it often got me into trouble. Now, however, instead of being reprimanded for speaking, I get paid to do it! That particular aspect of my personality turned out to be a gift in the long run, and it doesn't get any better than that.

The study of what makes us tick has been on going for some time now. From Sigmund Freud's theories and Carl Jung's teachings, to present-day psychology, the exploration into a human's inner self and personality continues, and for good reason. Our chances for happiness and success are greatly increased when we truly know ourselves well. It also helps us understand and communicate better with others. Suffice it to say, you will do your best career planning and skills assessment when you've become more self-aware and have learned how to apply it.

Remember that each of us has a personality that is as unique as our own fingerprints. It's what makes us who we are. It's what we like and don't like. It's what we believe in and what we doubt. We all have very specific preferences and values that affect the way we live and work.

Identifying these will not only help you understand yourself better, but will also greatly assist you in clarifying what it is you were meant to do.

The Myers Briggs Type Indicator (MBTI®)

Throughout my years as a career counsellor, I have taken a number of courses and have become certified in teaching specific assessment models geared towards better self-awareness. One of those models is the Myers Briggs Type Indicator (MBTI®). In use since 1962, MBTI® was developed by a mother-daughter team; Isabel Briggs and Katherine Myers. They based their work on the teachings of Carl Jung and constructed a questionnaire that identified personal preferences.

The intention of Myers-Briggs was to help people understand themselves and others better. Their contribution has been valuable in helping appreciate differences, communicate more effectively, and reduce interpersonal conflicts. Their model can help you understand why you find some people easy to be with whether working, talking, or playing, whereas with others it tends to be stressful or hard work; how you seem to be 'in sync' with some people and 'out of step' with others; how you quite consistently meet the expectations of some individuals and frequently disappoint others.

> The MBTI® provides a measure of personal "style" by examining eight preferences organized into four scales. The following is a brief overview of the stages:

Extroversion – Introversion

This scale describes how a person is energized. Extroverts prefer to draw their energy from the outside world of people and activities, whereas introverts prefer to draw energy from the internal world of ideas, emotions, or impressions.

Sensing – Intuition

This scale indicates what a person pays attention to when taking in information. A sensor prefers taking in information through the five senses and notices what is actual, while an intuitive uses the 'sixth sense' and wonders what might be.

Thinking – Feeling

This scale reflects what criteria a person uses for making decisions. A thinker/decider prefers to organize and structure decision-making information in a logical, objective way, whereas a feeling/decider prefers the personal, value-oriented method.

Judgement – Perception

This scale refers to what type of lifestyle people prefer. Judging-people have a preference for planned and organized lives, while perceiving-people prefer living spontaneous and flexible lives.

In the interest of space and time, I have elected to briefly touch on this subject but encourage you to further research and explore the Myers Briggs Type Indicator® and its questionnaire. I know that you will find it valuable in determining what your own preferences are and in learning how to apply them to your search for that dream career.

My adventure in life has brought me into contact with many special people who have all contributed in some way to the quest for better understanding ourselves and others, and how this all relates to our lives, our work, and our work environments. In 1997 I had a chance encounter with one such person. I had flown into Toronto from the Timmins, Ontario area after teaching a workshop there.

The flight had been delayed due to an ice storm we were experiencing. I didn't land until well after two a.m. and I was scheduled for an eight a.m. workshop in Sault St. Marie that morning, where I would be teaching people from all over the country. Needless to say, I just wanted to get to my hotel. It had been a trying evening, but it was about to take a most unexpected and pleasant turn.

I exited the airport and spotted a limo sitting out front. I am not a really shy person, especially when I could use a break, and I proceeded to ask the driver if he could possibly give me a lift. He said he would have to ask his occupant, who had hired the ride. This gentleman was gracious enough to agree.

That is how I was fortunate enough to meet Joseph Sherren, president of Ethos Enterprises Inc., trainers and consultants, and also the author of the book *iLead*[1]. He is a dynamic and popular speaker who was en route to the Laurentians the following day for a training session of his own. You can imagine my reaction when I discovered that we were both in quite similar fields, and I knew that there was probably much I could learn from this person. One of the most intriguing aspects that I took away from this meeting was my introduction to a concept Joe had developed regarding communication types. His research shows that we are preprogrammed at birth with a need to receive communication in a very specific way. It has to do with the alignment of our DNA within the MHC (Major Histocompatibility Complex) family.

The following information will give you amazing insight into what type of communication you most prefer and how to apply this to the way you communicate and deal with others. It will help you understand yourself better and hence, what type of employment for which you are best suited. It will also aid you in recognizing why others act the way they do; whether it be co-workers, management, or friends and family. It will aid you in your daily interaction with people as well enhancing your interview style when applying for a job.

As we begin to explore Joseph's concept, The Birds,™ you will come to understand the natural gifts you were given the day you came into the world. God has a plan for each and every one of us and has equipped us with the abilities we need to accomplish his purpose for our lives. All

---

[1] Sherren, Joseph. *iLead*. Blooming Twig Books. 2011. eBook

the gifts are equally important; none better than others. As the Bible states, "Together we have everything, alone we have nothing."

When I was younger, I often had conflict with my father. As a young child I didn't understand this, but later, as I started to study personality types, I realized he was the complete opposite to my personality type. We were both looking at the same picture but seeing different things.

Over the past twenty years that I have spent working with various organizations and helping people look for work, I started to notice that various personality types gravitated to different occupations. When you begin to reflect on your career path, considering your gifts is a critical step. You may be asking yourself, "What are natural gifts?" Wikipedia simply describes 'gifted' as an "intellectual ability." The best way I can describe a gift is that it is something you seem to be able to do effortlessly and people admire you for it. I believe that gifts are from God.

Once you identify and understand your gifts you will have a clearer idea of the occupations you will be suited for and that you will love. One of the best stories a client shared with me while I was a senior corporate trainer for a large organization helps to reinforce the importance of our gifts. I was working on a project that had a two-week deadline and the company had assigned someone to help me complete the project. One day this person said to me, "You know, I'm smarter than the average bear!" When I replied, "You are?" he proceeded to explain to me that he had gone to law school for seven years, had articled for a year, had written and passed the bar exam and then practised law for a year and a half before discovering he didn't like the occupation. He told me he wanted to do what I do for a living.

Imagine my surprise! Wow, he WAS right. That boy had a very high IQ and was able to learn something he ultimately didn't like. Still, it didn't guarantee him happiness or success. Then, a few years ago, I was at a meeting and shared that story. Someone in the room looked at me and told me that that was his story too. "Yeah, that's everyone's story," I replied. He went on to explain that it really was his story as he had been a lawyer and had left the occupation years ago because he hated going to work every day.

Another story that stood out to me was when one of my workshop clients explained how his son had chosen his career path. He had asked his son what the boy wanted to do upon graduating from high school. When the son's reply was one of uncertainty, the father suggested engineering. The son agreed and went off to school in the States to study engineering. After he had completed the first year, his father received his report card and was dismayed to find that his son had failed every course. Obviously upset, he called the boy, referred to the report he had received, and said, "Son, you are stupid and I have the proof."

I asked the gentleman how his son was doing now and was told that after three years of the course, his son had only actually successfully completed one year. Of course, the father was very angry because his son's education was costing him upwards of $23,000 U.S. per year.

But whose dream was this anyway? I'm thinking that I wouldn't want to be driving on a bridge or living in a building designed by this guy's son! The number of students that go to college or university without having a clear idea of who they are, continues to astound me. Understanding your personality is one of the keys to your success!

Take a pen and paper and write your name with your writing hand. Now, sign your name with your opposite hand. How did it feel when you wrote with your dominant hand? I'm sure it felt natural and effortless and you didn't have to think very hard about it. Now, consider how it felt when you did it with your other hand. It probably felt awkward, uncomfortable, and difficult, and you had to really concentrate at attempting to keep it from being a messy signature.

Let's say that you were unfortunate enough to break your dominant arm and were going to be in a cast for six months. You would start writing with your opposite hand and would quite likely become somewhat proficient after six months of practice. This ability would have developed in spite of yourself. This is similar to the stories I just shared with you. When your arm was fully healed, would you continue to write with your opposite hand? I'm thinking probably not, as we are creatures of habit. Personality and talent are the same. You may be able to do something, but that something may not be your preference and that is why eighty percent of the members of today's workforce are unsatisfied with their work.

Joseph Sherren's assessment will enable you to understand what is important to you, based on your personality type. I would like to extend my sincere thanks to Joe for sharing his wisdom and kindness and for allowing me to present his concept to you in this book.

Joe Sherren's "The Birds™"[2]

Effective communication begins with the act of giving part of yourself to the other person.

Over many years Joe had observed many things about the differences in the way people communicate. He had attended numerous seminars, read many books, conducted informal studies, and had even become certified to teach workshops on behavioural science. These resources were all designed to improve our understanding of each other's personalities and attitudes. But many of them often miss the most important point – the point being, how can we quickly identify and adapt our communication for a wide range of diverse individuals, in order to be more effective in achieving mutual goals?

Joe Sherren has spent fifteen years developing a model that he has used successfully to help people create powerful communication connections. We are presenting it here in the hope that it will help you develop skills in how to quickly identify, through a variety of signals, what another person requires from you when you are sending messages. Of course, the information is also intended to help you understand how to modify your style to one most suitable for the individuals you are trying to motivate, influence or change.

---

[2] Used with permission – Joseph Sherren

This document has been used as a supplementary take-away for participants who have attended Joe's high-impact, interactive seminar, "Creating Communication Connections." Those who participate in the seminar experience a series of scenarios, which in turn help them discover the primary strengths and weaknesses of how they communicate and interact with people of similar and different communication styles.

As many of us realize, the field of behavioural communication is not an exact science. Although there are those who will look for specific answers and a precise formula for developing better relationships, there are none. By utilizing many attitudinal studies and personality models developed over the last forty years, what we have been able to do, is to create a model that will give practitioners a higher probability of success in their communication effectiveness.

To make the concept simpler, easier to follow, and more efficient to relate, we have assigned each of the communication styles the name of a bird. The attributes of the bird closely relate to the communication style of the individuals who fall into that group. The four communication styles are:

- Eagle
- Dove
- Peacock
- Owl

Everyone will have a one, two, three, four communication-style sequence. For example, one would be your primary style, two your secondary style and so on, with the fourth being your weakest. Most people will have strong primary and secondary styles. Others may also have a third style, which might strongly influence the other two. We will outline the fundamental strengths and weaknesses of each of the styles as well as the more finite differences, depending on the order of the other influencing styles.

What follows is a communication analysis. Please circle the letter that reflects your number one choice in answer to each question.

A Communication Analysis

1. What is your preferred way of dressing?

    (E) Designer, classy, more formal
    (P) Bold colors, trendy, informal, lots of black
    (D) Gentle muted colors, casual, loose sweaters, track suits
    (O) Conservative, classic, practical, businesslike

2. In meetings, are you more...?

    (E) Direct and to the point
    (P) Animated, excitable, friendly
    (D) Inclined to dreamy thoughts, a peacemaker, casual
    (O) Specific, concise, accurate

3. Which of the following would be your preferred shape?

△	~	○	□
(E)	(P)	(D)	(O)

4. When making critical decisions, do you require...?

    (E) Options for various courses of action
    (P) Testimonials from trusted others
    (D) Assurances and support
    (O) Evidence and proof

5. If given free choice, where would you most prefer to live?

    (E) Suburban palace; two-story, four-bedroom with paved driveway
    (P) Country home on acreage with friendly neighbours
    (D) Cabin in the woods with peace and tranquility
    (O) Condo or townhouse in a downtown area, and eating out a lot

6. Your most favoured vacation would be?

   (E) Adventures and travel
   (P) Caribbean resort – sun, sand, lounging
   (D) At home or at a cottage – rest, reading, and friends
   (O) Organized city or country tour

7. When attending a seminar, you would prefer...?

   (E) Practical information that is brief and summarized – few workshops
   (P) Lots of fun learning, jokes, and analogies
   (D) Comfortable, low-pressure environment – no role playing
   (O) Logically Laid out, not ambiguous information, follow the agenda

8. Which of the following motivates you more than the others?

   (E) Getting and seeing results
   (P) Recognition and applause
   (D) Personal attention and friendship
   (O) Lots of organized activity going on

9. Is your office more...?

   (E) Neat and organized
   (P) Disorganized with fun stuff – files in piles
   (D) Friendly with comfortable chairs and personal pictures
   (O) Working environment, laid out and practical – wall board

10. Your preferred way to sleep?

    (E) On your back, straight out
    (P) In a cuddling or almost foetal position
    (D) On your side with your knees slightly bent
    (O) On your stomach with your arms up by your head

11. Are you more...?

   (E) Highly assertive and reserved
   (P) Highly assertive and outgoing
   (D) Less assertive and outgoing
   (O) Less assertive and reserved

12. An appropriate summary of your strengths, not the role you play in your profession, would be?

   (E) Getting to the bottom line of complex problems, and making critical decisions
   (P) Seeing the bigger picture, conceptualizing, using your intuition, and being creative
   (D) Interpersonal relationships, helping others get along, expressing feelings as comfortably as ideas, working teams.
   (O) Establishing standards, maintaining self-discipline, admiring others who maintain a sense of discipline and quality about their work.

What this survey is designed to do is determine your primary and your secondary strengths in the area of communication. In this test, the letters are represented as follows:

   (E) = Eagle Quantity_____
   (D) = Dove Quantity_____
   (P) = Peacock Quantity_____
   (O) = Owl Quantity_____

Count up the scores in each of the letters and order from the highest to the lowest. This will give you an indication of your preferred way of communicating.

Birds of a Feather

These birds have certain characteristics and behaviours, which we associate with them. We find that in the communication process, people also exhibit similar characteristics – and we can relate them to each of these birds. In short, the people to whom we assign each of the styles appear to share similar characteristics with the respective birds.

Just as bird watchers delight in watching birds and their behaviours, you will enjoy watching for these "birds" among your friends, family and professional acquaintances.

The Eagle

Eagles can be quickly recognized by their very serious, concentrated, and stern look when you are communicating with them. They can stare at you for long periods of time without blinking. They normally have short, neat hair. Their clothes are quite tidy and tucked in, and even in casual situations, will have a professional flair to them.

When answering the phone they will just say things like, "Bill here," or "This is Sam." If they are in charge, even their answering machine greetings are quick and to the point. When they leave messages for others they will just say, "This is Bill, call me."

Generally, Eagles like their information presented to them in a bottom-line and netted-out fashion. When speaking with them, be brief and direct, stick to business, and assure them that results will achieved. Focus on what you want and how you want it.

Strengths associated with Eagles are their ability to make decisions, even critical ones, quite quickly. They can adapt quickly to change and like to take on new challenges. They feel there is no obstacle that can't be overcome and they are usually optimistic about the future.

Eagles do have some weaknesses. They will often put results ahead of other people's feelings. They seem to always be in a hurry – they are not very patient and will cut you off, if you do not get to the point very quickly. They will often give you an answer, before you have finished asking your question.

Sometimes, they appear to push people around, are regarded as poor listeners, and certainly do not like working in teams unless they are in charge. Do not expect them to express personal feelings if you do not know them well. They might become preoccupied with other matters if you start rambling on during a conversation.

When we ask them to choose between four shapes – circle, triangle, squiggle, or square – the Eagle will select the triangle. This is a pointed wedge shape, which can push further and release greater energy than any other form. It has been said that people who choose the triangle first, tend to be preoccupied with sexual thoughts and see themselves as being great lovers.

In a study at the Yale University Child Development Clinic, it was observed that the triangle symbol required a more developed connection between the brain and hand. The normal child did not draw this form until the age of five, though the circle and square were accomplished at three and four years of age.

Children who are Eagles tend to be aggressive and energetic. In drawings they might depict steeples, airplanes, and sailboats. Their doodling will have many pointy figures in it. Even their handwriting will be hard on the paper with strong points in it.

Experiments at Yale University and at McGill University in Montreal have indicated that emotions are affected by the action in the hypothalamus in the center of the brain. By electrically stimulating this portion of the brain, responses of love, hate, fear, aggressiveness, and sex have been evoked. Aggressiveness is closely identified with the sex urge, since they both produce a high degree of excitation and people experiencing them seek active outlets for this energy. So, as children or adults, if these people are not able to satisfy one of these urges, they will replace it with another.

Sigmund Freud made reference to the triangle as being a phallic symbol, representing the sexual organs of the male and female. It has been said that the sexual instinct is the most powerful human motivator. If this energy is not released, however, it can also cause unhealthy behaviours.

Eagles are sharp thinkers and have keen perception. They will arrive at solutions quickly. Independent thinkers, they resist being placed in any position subordinate to others. They have the ability to work independently and that's what they enjoy.

Eagles can be emotional, but are not sensitive or compassionate to the emotional needs of others. They are direct, and like to get to the point quickly. Most people like and admire Eagles from a distance, but are apprehensive about approaching them on an intimate basis.

When communicating with Eagles, be brief and direct; they want you to get to the point with no frills. Focus on what you want, and let them have control. Do not waste their time with details because they grasp broad concepts quickly and will quickly turn off.

Eagles like to learn by trying out ideas, theories, and techniques to see if they work in practice. Consequently, they visualize new ideas and look for opportunities to try them. For example, they often return from a conference or workshop excited about new ideas and eager to take some related action right away. Eagles like to get on with things and tend to act quickly and confidently on any idea that captures their interest.

They tend to be impatient with touch-feely discussions, and any talk that does not come to a fast conclusion. They are practical, down-to-earth people who like making fast decisions and solving complex problems. Eagles see problems and opportunities as a challenge. Their philosophy is: "There is always a better way," and "If it works, that's what matters."

When sleeping, Eagles like to be on their backs – straight out, and they take up lots of space. They prefer to live in the typical suburban palace; two-story four-bedroom house, with a circular driveway. To please them, it should have a formal dining area and a paved driveway with a fancy car and lawn sprinklers. When entertaining, they are likely to plan the event well in advance to ensure that it goes smoothly. They like it to be professional and organized and would prefer it on the patio

– garden-style with tablecloth and wine – or in a formal dining room with silver.

For vacations, Eagles prefer adventure and action. Whether it is camping in the wilderness, hiking, fishing, skiing, golf, or even white water rafting, they like to be active and not sit around. To them it is a waste of a vacation to do nothing.

Their offices are often neat and organized with their qualifications, trophies, and certificates of achievement on display. If possible, they have their large power furniture arranged in an "I'm in charge here" layout.

As we noted, everyone has both a primary and secondary style of receiving communication. If we can recognize and remember this idea, we could possibly increase our effectiveness by as much as seventy-five percent.

Eagle-Doves

Eagle-Dove combinations are self-motivated individuals with an inexhaustible supply of energy that constantly needs to be released. People are important to those who exhibit this combination. Their need to give love is greater than their need to receive it. In associations with others they become the givers rather than the takers.

Eagle-Doves want to take action quickly and will not wait around for somebody else to make a move or to come up with an idea. They enjoy competition and challenges and they do not discourage easily.

Eagle-Doves have quick minds and frequently act on impulse and intuition. Projects that tend to go on for a long time begin to bore the Eagle involved in them, because Eagles constantly like new challenges.

Sometimes they can be understanding and compassionate, but that trait is often overruled by their impatient urge to get on with the job. One problem with the Eagle-Dove combination is that they develop internal stress from their conflicting impulses. On one hand, they are sensitive to the feelings of others. On the other hand, they just want to get on with it and will walk over people to get to where they want to go.

Then, because of the Dove influence, they will feel bad about what they have done.

They will become easily upset by others who do not treat them fairly, and will lose their tempers quickly. However, they will just as quickly forgive and carry on, as if nothing has happened.

Eagle-Owls

Eagle-Owl individuals are more left-brain than those with other combinations. They are not into self-appreciation, and that quality also makes them much easier people to live with than some of the other types. Rather than Eagle-Owls being emotionally fed by others, their aggressive energy leads them to look for constructive outlets that depend more upon their skills and abilities.

They are able to evaluate a situation quickly, using reason and logic, and they make the decisions necessary to resolve it. Normally, they do not allow emotions to interfere with reason. They are realistic, with both feet on the ground, and do not waste time fantasizing or daydreaming.

Eagle-Owl combinations with Dove dominance are able to experience more creative thought. They will occasionally find the time to look for romance and idealism in the things they do.

Eagle-Peacocks

With Eagle-Peacocks, you must get to the facts very quickly and not waste time when communicating with them. For best results, you must immediately become very personable. It would be wise to show them that you also appreciate fun in life and to even fit a joke into the conversation.

They are highly independent and individualistic people. They have great power of imagination and possess highly aggressive energy that gives them unlimited scope for expression. They can be stimulated both by facts and imagination, and will use this combination to artistically express themselves.

Eagle-Peacocks have a great desire to leave their marks on the universe and to contribute to improving society in some way. However, they also want the recognition for doing it before they die.

If these people have a dominant Owl trait, they are more conscious of a need to feel secure in actual living situations. Because of the combination, they conform and live by the rules of society more easily.

If their dominant third style is Dove, they will want to be very sensitive to others, but at the same time, will not let anyone get in the way of them achieving their goals. They have a need to connect and be close to others, but usually end up with only a few close friends.

The Peacock

Peacocks can be recognized by their bright clothes and big, friendly grins. They usually have a twinkle in their eyes that makes people wonder what they are up to, or what mischievous thoughts they are having. While some people may have a "bad hair day," Peacocks have a "bad hair life." No matter what they do, they seem never to be satisfied with how their hair turns out.

When answering the phone, their voices and words are optimistic and cheerful. When you ask how they are, they will always answer "great," "wonderful," or "sensational," or provide some other lively response. They will usually sound truly pleased to talk to you.

With great imaginations, they can be very creative, and behave optimistically in most situations. They get along fabulously with people, and have a charisma that attracts others to them instantly. They are never at a loss for words in a social situation.

In their natural state, they are outgoing, spontaneous, and highly expressive. You can recognize them by their clothes because they usually go for bright and fancy colours, but they also have strong leanings towards wearing black. Although they are very enthusiastic, they will react quickly to any perceived threat. Their main mission is to enjoy life.

On the negative side, they will interrupt when you are speaking and tend to exaggerate. If they listen at all, it is only to see when you are going to stop talking so they know when to start. They are poor time managers and often arrive at meetings late. They like new projects but become bored quickly and go looking for something else. They do not like detailed work and may not follow through on important items, which causes them problems with their work.

The symbol that tends to attract Peacocks first is the squiggle. This is even apparent in their handwriting, which is usually hard to read, and does not always stay on the line. The squiggle is the symbol of imagination and creativity. These are some of their dominant characteristics and they bring their creativity and open-mindedness to all aspects of their lives. While many of their ideas could never be implemented, they are fascinating to hear and to debate.

Their imaginations are stimulated by an intense desire to see and know more. They do not generally accept the status quo, and like to go off on adventures in search of new discoveries.

Sometimes they are not in touch with reality. Much of their thinking time is spent in higher thought, beyond the boring existence of everyday living.

They can be aggressive, especially if they have a strong Eagle presence. When their natural ability to be imaginative is suppressed, there will probably be negative consequences for the person who gets in their way. Peacocks must channel their energy into constructive activity. If this does not happen, they may become withdrawn or aggressive. They seem to be always searching for excitement and to others may not always appear to have two feet firmly on the ground.

When communicating with Peacocks, make it fun and stimulating and remember to smile. Use analogies for description – and place them as the most important person in the interaction; they thrive on public recognition. If you are trying to sell them on an idea or concept, arrange it so they will be recognized for their great insights and perception. Allow them to verbalize their ideas and visions.

In the learning process, Peacocks involve themselves in new experiences fully and without reservation. They enjoy the here and now and are happy to be dominated by immediate experiences. They are open-minded, not sceptical, and this tends to make them enthusiastic about anything new. Their philosophy is: "I'll try anything once." They tend to act first and consider the consequences later. Their days are filled with thought and activity.

Peacocks will tackle problems by brainstorming. As soon as the excitement from one activity has died down, they are busy looking for the next. They thrive on the challenge of new experiences, but are bored with implementation and maintaining over the longer-term consolidation. They are gregarious people, constantly involving themselves with others, but in doing so, always put themselves at the center of all activity.

Peacocks prefer to sleep in the more foetal position. Whether their sleepmates be people, pillows, or pets, they like to cuddle. They would prefer living in a country home on an acreage; perhaps have horses or other animals; and to spend their leisure time visiting and joking with friendly neighbours.

For vacations, they like to get away to a Caribbean beach resort. They love to spend most of their time in the sun; resting, relaxing and talking to people at the swim-up pool bar.

Their offices are usually cluttered. They will have toys and cartoons. Much of the time they will have files sitting around in piles. Once in awhile they will make an effort to clean it up, but to no avail. In the end, it just returns to the way it was.

Peacock-Doves

When communicating with Peacock-Doves, make sure that after your initial friendliness, you follow up with accurate and appropriate facts and details. These people are both dreamy and realistic at the same time. They will mentally wander into their imaginations, then wake up to the safer practicalities of the real world. Their openness to new ideas and their willingness to see and accept change can work positively in developing an inherent ability to adjust to change.

Since their need for security is also very strong, they try to keep both feet on the ground consistently enough to function as members of the social environment. Home may be important, but variety and change are needed to keep them excited. If strong Eagle tendencies are present, they could become hostile and foster resentment, especially when they are interrupted or held back.

They are more involved with themselves than with other people. Personal relationships might take a backseat to other interests. Even family is more a means of securing their need for home stability, than for exchanging personal love. They are not easily influenced by other people or emotional attachments.

Peacock-Eagles

Peacock-Eagles are dynamic individuals who possess all the qualities for success and leadership. Their minds are never at rest, and they can never seem to stop thinking and planning. They take laptop computers on vacation, because their minds are in high gear all the time.

They have an ability to conceptualize and bring abstract ideas into focus with accurate comprehension. Their ability to do it usually results in solid theories. They can absorb knowledge and understand abstract concepts without working at it too hard. However, they expect others to follow through with details of their projects, because they become bored with follow-up and detailed procedures.

These people are great at being able to conceptualize, create, and develop solutions. However, do not expect them to be around when it comes to actually implanting the solutions.

Challenges are a source of stimulation and pleasure. They search for a variety of areas where they can discharge their mental energies, which are continuously building up as they are being released. Although receptive to new ideas, they will not be led down the garden path by ideas that do not conform to some sort of intelligent order.

In relationships, these people are either envied or idolized. Unfortunately, they do not make the ideal companions or mates, because they spend little time developing interpersonal relationships and are quite intolerant of the weaknesses of others. They have a strong need for companionship; consciously or unconsciously finding relationships with people who have similar values. Security is not a strong motivator for these people, and they are unable to truly relax and enjoy the company of others.

Those with a strong Owl influence are even less motivated to develop strong relationships and they have little compassion and patience with others. They do not suffer fools gladly. They will resist social situations and shy away from being part of a group. Very little of their free time is devoted to parties or play, and even humour must be sprinkled with provocative thought to be appealing.

The Dove

Doves can be spotted by their sincere, friendly smiles, their warm eyes, their loose, untucked clothing, and comfortable postures. They will have relaxed handshakes, and they will buy shoes for comfort rather than style. The symbol they are most often drawn to is the circle, which represents peace, love, and harmony. Doves are very much into tranquility and pursue it in all areas of their lives.

Their handwriting tends to be rounded, with emphasis being on a circular motion, and curls at the end of words. To understand why the circle is referred to as the symbol of love, think of pleasure items that are round, soft, and warm. For a child, it is a rattle, a ball, and a mother's warm breast, which are a comfort and delight. Doves prefer objects with no sharp edges to hurt them. They respond to round, smooth objects, which sooth, pacify, and provide safe play. The preference is reflected in the Doves' behaviour. They do not like violence, will run away from a fight, shrink at the sight of an accident, and find tense arguments distressing. What Doves seek mostly is affection and approval, which they find in non-threatening situations. They tend not to be hostile or aggressive, and would rather play than fight. Doves do have a tendency to be possessive and jealous about people who are close to them, as well as about items that bring them pleasure.

When communicating with Doves, you must be sincere in your approach, agreeable, and supportive. You must not come on too strong or in a panic. Focus on what you want and how you want it. Be patient with them and give them time to adjust their thinking, to allow them to respond appropriately. If you can make a personal connection with someone they know and trust, they will more likely listen to you and absorb what you are saying.

Their voice mail usually says something like, "Good morning, this is Sally, I'm sorry I am not here to take your call. Your call is very important to me. Please leave your name and number and I will be sure to get back to you as soon as I can."

When learning, Doves like to stand back to ponder experiences and observe from many different perspectives. They collect data, both first-hand and from others, and prefer to think about it thoroughly before coming to any conclusion. They tend to postpone reaching and announcing definitive conclusions for as long as possible.

Their operating philosophy is to be cautious. Doves are thoughtful people who like to consider all possible angles and implications before making a move. They prefer to take a back seat in meetings and discussions. They enjoy observing other people in action. They listen to others and get the drift of the discussion before making their own points. Doves tend to adopt a low profile and have a quiet, tolerant, relaxed air about them. When they react, they consider the whole picture, which includes the sum total of all their experiences and observations.

Other characteristics of Doves include their tendency to sleep on their sides in the spoon position – and the fact that they would prefer the tranquility of living in a cabin in the woods and enjoying their solitude, to city living. They enjoy being independent, watching sunsets, relaxing, floating around in paddleboats, and having their families and close friends accessible when necessary.

They often prefer a vacation at someone's home or cottage where they can sleep in, catch up on their reading, see some friends, and visit family. At work, even their offices have a friendly atmosphere and are decorated with pictures and comfortable chairs. When co-workers come to them for favours, they have a hard time saying no, and people often take advantage of them. Other people sometimes see their friendly and accommodating natures as weakness and will try to exploit their loyalty.

Doves are warm and friendly people who listen actively and are very patient. They value personal relationships above all. They can be articulate and organized, and they work cohesively with others. They really like to work in areas with others who get along. You can always count on Doves, when they give you their word. They have good counselling skills and are usually known around the office as peacemakers, because they like to help others.

In meetings, Doves do not always push for what they want. When making decisions, they solicit input from as many people they can. They often know what the decision is going to be, but input from others helps confirm what they already know.

When you first meet Doves, you should not come on too strong. The behaviour will remind them of a used-car salesman and they will back off. They are very trusting, get let down by people, and worry too much about what others think.

They do not like change that people have not had time to get used to and accept. They spend too much personal time doing things for others. Doves avoid taking risks and avoid conflict at all cost. They wait too long to act, and will hold a grudge against anyone who has done them wrong in the past.

Dove-Owls

Dove-Owls who have Eagle dominance are highly motivated by love and the desire to share it. They will try to secure that love by creating an infrastructure of family, home, and a circle of friends. They will guard against any outside threat that might disturb the lifestyle they have put together. Their strong desire for love often manifests itself in their quest for achievement and in a strong sexual drive. Because of the opposing nature of these styles (Dove-Eagle), these individuals may cause themselves internal stress in their relationships with other people.

Those with Peacock dominance are very similar, except they combine all this with lofty visions of great accomplishments. Although the need for security is highest in their motivation, they first must achieve a loving, secure relationship. Normally, they do not focus on completing pragmatic goals, other than creating a comfortable family home. They tend to avoid fights and do their best to stay away from situations involving conflict. Their large capacities for pleasure, combined with their creative natures, cause them to go out of their way in trying to bring happiness to lots of people.

Dove-Peacocks

Dove-Peacocks with strong Owl attributes have two extremes to their nature. One is that they take the time to be playful, compassionate, and enjoy the pleasure of being with people. The other is an aggressive drive to get ahead without the interference of feelings that might slow them down. Unfortunately, the two extremes could ultimately come together and serve to conceal their inner feelings. Many are realists with both feet on the ground. They search for a profound love with another individual to satisfy their every emotion and desire. They are extremely imaginative and will unconsciously invent an unreal image of others. This quality opens them up to possible disillusionments and disappointments.

Wealth and social success are of less concern than other values, since they are interested in attaining loftier goals to satisfy their needs.

To be successful in an artistic endeavour, they must have someone they can trust to represent them and protect them in the world.

Dove-Peacocks who have the spirit of an Eagle are more aggressive in their search for romance and more ambitious in finding outlets for their creative abilities. They will also stand up to other people who threaten their ideals and principles, and will fight for the principle of personal rights.

Dove-Eagles

Dove-Eagles with Peacock tendencies are motivated by the desire for love, which is also a major factor behind their sexual motivation and drive for success. They might have a touch of romanticism and frequent fantasies.

They are not concerned with financial security. These people are not afraid to face problems, and will focus on resolving them. Freedom always comes before safety. The best security for them is the freedom to express their feelings and abilities.

Often they will experience internal stress because their Dove traits will cause them to be sensitive to others. However, when the Eagle nature in them takes over, they will walk over anyone who gets in their way. Then, as a Dove, they will feel really bad because they hurt someone else's feelings. At times, as they think about it, they will not like themselves.

The Owl

Owls can be recognized by their cross-looking demeanours. In fact, many will experience people coming up to them saying, "Are you angry at me for some reason? Have I done something to offend you?"

Even as children, Owls will often pout if things are not going their way. Their hair and clothes are practical, and they normally check the weather or the day's agenda before getting dressed.

You will find that many Owls have trouble looking at you directly in the eye and holding your gaze for a period of time without blinking. As children, a higher proportion of them wear glasses.

Their voice mail greetings will usually be a variation on, "Good morning, this is Tuesday, May, the second. I will be out of my office attending meetings until 11:00 a.m. I, then, plan to… (and so on). Please leave your name, number, time of your call and the reason… blah, blah."

Their primary symbol choice is the square, which reflects a strong desire for security. For confirmation, look at how often the squareness appears in their handwriting. This shape came into their lives the first time they were placed in a crib as an infant. It kept them safe and secure. Later, a playpen that was larger, but still square, protected them from harm. They liked to play with blocks, and as their intelligence developed, they placed one on top of the other, building structures.

Because of their focus on security, their homes are their castles. Whether it is gardening, taking care of repairs and improvements, entertaining in the home, or generally puttering around, they are comfortable and content in a home situation. They like working with their hands and like to build things. Their gift of patience helps them follow through each step of a project until it's completed with accuracy. When this is carried to an extreme, it will cause them to develop perfectionist or conventional behaviours later in life.

Owls are both logical and practical, and they accumulate information that can be useful. Abstract thinking is not natural and they do not indulge in romantic or idealistic visions. These people have RRSPs for themselves as soon as they start work and RESPs for their children soon after their offspring are born. Sometimes they actually purchase a home before they get married and pay off the mortgage prior to having children.

Owls learn by adapting and integrating what is being communicated into complex, but logically sound theories. They think problems through in a step-by-step and pragmatic manner. They tend to come across as perfectionists who will not rest easily until things are tidy and fit into a rational scheme.

Owls are interested in basic assumptions, principles, theories, models, and systems. Their philosophy is: "Does this make sense?" and "How does this fit with that?"

Although very sensitive to other individuals, Owls will come across as detached, analytical, and dedicated to objectivity rather than anything approaching subjective, ambiguous, or touch-feely. Their approach to problems is consistently logical. This is their mindset and they rigidly reject anything that does not fit with it.

When sleeping, Owls prefer to lie on their stomachs with their arms up by their heads. They tend to gravitate to a lifestyle of condominium living in an urban setting where they can eat out, travel, shop, and attend theatre, musicals, and social events.

They will usually plan their vacations well in advance and select organized tours of cities and countries. They will attend museums, galleries, cafes, and concerts in the hope of learning new things.

Their offices will display an air of conservatism and have all the tools for working, such as a clock, wall chart, whiteboard, graphs, a barometer, and at the very least, a desk organizer. They adhere to their to-do lists religiously and usually have one for work, one for home, and sometimes others. We actually have met one who had a list of his to-do lists!

Owls are logical and very self-disciplined. They easily assimilate information accurately. They focus on quality and admire people with high standards regarding their work and lives. Their opinions are well thought-out and they make decisions primarily based on facts. They have a knack for problem solving and manage their time well. They are analytical and patient and come across as calm and rational, even though, internally, they may not be. They prefer a task-oriented environment and pride themselves on being precise and accurate. They are most comfortable when there are rules or guidelines to follow.

Owl weaknesses include getting stuck in an either/or mindset and they do not like getting involved in emotional or sensitive situations.

They come across as impersonal, even though they are very personable. It is common for Owls to lose sight of the big picture. They avoid confrontation, taking risks, or making fast decisions. In critical situations they will put right-versus-wrong ahead of other people's feelings.

They are not usually team players and can become defensive when criticized. They have a view of certain standards and strive to meet those whenever possible.

When communicating with an Owl, you must be thoroughly prepared and provide lots of accurate detail in a persistent, but relaxed, manner. Focus on what you want and why you want it. Prior to concluding a conversation, you should check for clarity of understanding.

Owl-Doves

The Owl-Doves with Eagle strengths like to feel safe and secure. When reaching for a goal they make sure they can achieve it; otherwise they will not reach for it at all. Their homes are their most valued possessions, along with everything contained within them. They will not indulge in any pleasure if it jeopardizes the stability and security of home and family life. Their view of love is that it belongs with the family unit, and even if it is lacking there, they will not compensate for it elsewhere. They like the comfort of culture and tradition, and enjoy friends and family. As peace-loving individuals, they dislike violence.

Owl-Doves can be counted on to be reasonable and logical in living situations, and will compromise in order to satisfy others. Their thoughts and actions are based on what they believe is practical. They rarely act on emotion alone, and quite often feel that they live a dull existence.

When Owl-Doves have Peacock dominance, they will glamorize love interests and home situations so that these objects become their source of pleasure and a means to satisfy their need for security. These people are even less ambitious and competitive than their related combinations, and will not struggle for fame or worldly gain beyond what is required for comfortable living. They enjoy simple pleasures, which are easily accessible.

Owl-Eagles

Owl-Eagles with Dove leanings will take aggressive action to ensure the security of self and family, and are willing to compete and fight for it. They are intelligent, and their approach to problems is both perceptive and logical. These qualities cause them to act first on reason rather than emotion – making them winners more often than losers. They work hard to provide good lifestyles for their families.

They believe in authority and discipline in both the home and in business, and are not easily swayed by emotion or hard-luck stories. They do not spend much time dreaming or fantasizing.

Those with Peacock strengths are more imaginative than some of the other types and will add a touch of creative thought to the things in which they participate. They are serious-minded, and intent upon keeping emotions under control. They do not need to have their egos stroked by others, and will seek security and self-actualization from personal accomplishments.

Owl-Peacocks

Owl-Peacocks are not easy people to understand or live with, because there are two strongly opposing factors guiding them. On one hand, they respond to practical reasoning and logic. On the other hand, their urge for exciting and romantic lives is strong. Consequently, the conflict causes them internal conflict and stress. Living a routine existence creates great frustration for them, and they might rebel against the lack of change in their lives. Conversely, they are not always aggressive enough to make these changes in their own lives. Picture an individual who wants to purchase a new home but cannot make the decision to sell the old one or put in an offer on the new one, and you will see Owl-Peacock with an Eagle's strength.

These people have ideas that are constructed on a solid base, even though imagination may sweep them away on wild tangents. They have an ability to put challenge in perspective, and use their imaginations to develop practical solutions. We have known people of this combination to make several home moves – from living in the city, to the country, and then back to the city. Their ideal life would be to live in a condo during the week, and have a country home for weekends and summers.

These people are not interested in developing close relationships with other people, because it is not a source of pleasure for them. Owl-Peacocks admire others who demonstrate high values. Their desire would be to be able to balance the real world and their dreams.

Flying on Your Own

Once you have learned the strengths and the weaknesses of each of these birds, and how to instantly recognize them, you will be able to adapt your communication style to be more effective when dealing with them. Understanding these differences will also mean that, from now on, you will be able to appreciate and like almost everyone you meet. You will be able to understand their differing needs and styles. And it is a given that people are just different.

This insight into the birds will also enable you to understand how people may behave at work or at social functions, how they approach risk-taking, or how they will likely respond to certain stresses. This will help you choose how to approach them in a sale and how to deal with them as customers, or even in a relationship situation,.

Communication is all about understanding and being understood. Familiarity with the nature of these birds will provide the insights to help you understand and be understood by others – a healthy and happy situation from any perspective.

The Value of Knowing What You Value

I hope you found Joe Sherren's Birds as interesting and helpful as I have. Get to know which bird best represents your own personality. This insight will aid you in understanding yourself better and therefore assist you in defining career goals. As stated earlier, it will also help you with your communication skills and with your overall interaction with others. On a personal note, for those who may be curious as to my own personality, I am primarily a Dove-Peacock with some Owl-Eagle secondary traits.

Another important aspect to keep in mind when considering what kind of occupation you are best suited for, is what values you hold dear. If you are working in an environment where your values are not supported, you will not be content or be able to flourish in your employment situation. For instance, if you highly value an atmosphere of teamwork and it is nonexistent in your job, you will more than likely be uninspired and lack motivation in your work. If you covet advancement in your occupation but are employed in a company where promotion or progress is unlikely, it will obviously have a negative affect on your overall view of the job.

In workshops I have taught during my career, I have used an exercise that I like to open with. It concerns personal values and just how much monetary value my clients might place on them by way of an 'auction sheet.' The clients are given a certain amount of 'money' and asked to budget on different personal values such as a satisfying and fulfilling marriage, or freedom to do what they want. Then, to ascertain just how important the values are to them, they are asked to bid on them in a make-believe auction. Most people find it helpful in ascertaining just what they value most out of life.

A similar assessment tool that you can use as an individual is the Work Values Inventory. It is a list of values that are split into the following four categories: Core values that are important to you in your life; work environment values; work interaction values; and work activity values. Each category offers several related values for you to assess as;

always important to you; sometimes important; and not important to you. It is an excellent way of determining what values are of high priority to you in your life and work. I encourage you to find it online and actually complete the assessment. I could have included the entire exercise here, but I feel that an important part of your search for that optimum career is to be personally proactive, including doing your own reading and research beyond the information in this book.

Also, it is important to remember that if there is a specific company you are interested in working for, that company's values should be in alignment with your own for you to be assured of having job fulfillment. Research the company and ascertain if they have a mission statement and what that statement says. It is a good reflection of the company's overall values.

Remember that selecting career options that best coincide with your values will give you better probability for success and fulfillment in that chosen field. You should also take into account that your work values may actually change as work situations change, so it is imperative to review and evaluate your work values often.

Values and Goals and How They Have Affected My Own Career Path

I think it is important to include stories from my life so that this book is more than just a self help-type read. I want you to be able to envision a face behind the teachings and understand the personal aspect of it all. It hasn't always been easy for me and I've been in similar positions that many of you may have been in when it came to trying to figure out what I was best suited to do, and how to deal with work situations that weren't offering me the best opportunity for growth and contentment.

Let me start by saying that one of the most important values I hold dear to my heart is the ability to help others. A great part of the pleasure I get from my job comes from the fulfillment of that value and the fact that my work is all about teaching and guiding people in need of clarification when it comes to career paths. The rewards for me seem to be never-ending and few things bring me more joy than seeing someone succeed in finding the right occupation.

After graduating from high school and pondering what it was I wanted to do with my life, I set my sights on teaching little ones and applied to college for Early Childhood Education. Unfortunately, the course enrolment was full and so, instead of sticking to my original career goal, I enrolled in the Bilingual Secretary program. This turned out to be a huge mistake. About the only thing I had going for me in that particular job was the fact that I was bilingual. Every other aspect of it was not suited to my interests or values and I was very unhappy doing it.

Eventually I wound up in early childhood education and I enjoyed teaching little ones, but other circumstances led me to continue my career quest and I landed a job with the government as a counsellor with Human Resources Department Canada.

I thoroughly enjoyed my role at HRDC, teaching people who had filed for employment assistance. However, at one point during my employment I was moved to the position of adjudicator where I dealt more with employment assistance applications and paperwork than actually having a hands-on role with the public. Needless to say, I couldn't come close to processing the number of applications expected of me. It just wasn't my cup of tea, and I was miserable. It wasn't until I returned to my role of speaking to and guiding people that I got back on track with what I was clearly meant to do.

I hope that these personal examples will give you a clearer idea of just how important it is to stay true to your interests and values when considering what it is you want to do for a living. Knowing the traits that make up your personality is vital to successfully reaching that destination of a career that fulfills all your needs and wants.

chapter 3

WILL THE LABOUR MARKET SUPPORT MY CHOICE?

Identifying Employment Availability

We live in a world of changing trends…fashion trends, dance and music trends, and technological trends, to name a few. It is important to be aware that the labour market is no different and that it experiences trends of its own. The late Dick Clark was a producer of a variety of music shows, game shows, and movies. Perhaps he was best known as the host of *American Bandstand* and *New Year's Rockin' Eve*. He once said, "I don't make trends. I just find out what they are and exploit them." When determining your career path it is important to be informed about the labour market and its trends, both present and future, and whether the occupation you've set your sights on will be accessible.

Researching the job market and understanding future employment trends will aid you in making well-informed career decisions. If tomorrow's opportunities do not include the career you intend to pursue then you will be setting yourself up for failure. Research will show you that certain sectors are experiencing growth while others are facing declines. Future job market structure is affected by a variety of factors such as technology, population growth, and consumer demand, as well as economic growth.

Alvin Toffler, the American writer and futurist who authored the book *Future Shock* in 1970, is a man who follows economic and demographic trends in an attempt to predict the future. He states that there have been three major ages or revolutions, which have affected how people earn a living: the Agricultural Age, which transitioned into the Industrial Revolution, which in turn changed into the current trend, the Information Age.

He contends that the Industrial Age concepts, where the company takes care of the employee are fading away. Life-long employment is no longer guaranteed, nor is a pension plan, as many companies are no longer providing retirement funds and are also moving away from covering medical expenses. Toffler's projection for the future of employment is that self-employment and working from home will be large trends in the Information Age.

Certainly, one cannot overlook the major impact that the introduction of the computer has had on the employment market and its future, as the advancements continue today. Scientific and technical-services sectors are seeing growth concerning computer systems design and related services, due to the increasing use of information technology and the need to maintain system and network security.

Research suggests that because of today's aging population, the trend appears to support the move from employment in the goods-producing industry to services-providing jobs. Not only are the Baby Boomers reaching retirement age, but they are also living longer because of advancement in medicine and health technologies, not to mention an increased awareness of nutrition and the move towards living a healthier lifestyle.

As one generation faces retirement the members of another enter educational institutions, in hopes of earning certificates and diplomas that will prepare them to fill jobs vacated by the retiring public. This, of course, will also have an effect on the future of the service-providing positions related to education. Information-sector employment growth will be most evident in computer-related industries such as software publishing, Internet publishing, and wireless communication. I have mentioned the previous conditions to give you a little better idea about how the changing world has affected the labour market and how it will continue to impact employment trends.

I encourage you to take the time to consider and even write about world events that you think have had a profound impact on the labour force and what exactly that impact was. After that, look at current events and advancements and consider how they relate to employment and the possible growth or decline in certain occupations in the future. For instance, take into account that in 1870 a US Census concluded that women made up only fifteen percent of the total workforce at that time (1.8 million out of an estimated 12.5 million). The advent of world wars eventually saw a need for more women to be employed because of the manufacturing of military-related items such as weapons, but also to fill many positions that had been vacated by the men who went to war. Later on, it was the feminist movement in 1960 that led to a greater increase in women entering the workforce, which in turn lead to the need for an increase in daycares and early childhood education.

Keeping yourself informed about current events and employment trends will aid you a great deal with your search for the right occupation. Settling on one choice that best suits your personality, interests, and talents may have to be re-examined if there are no jobs out there for you. This doesn't mean that you will never be able to realize your goal. Remember that the world is constantly changing, as are the trends that make some jobs available and others not so much. What may not be an opportunity right now can easily become a reality in the future, so don't let go of that dream. You may just have to experience a detour in the journey or a postponement of a goal if that's what you have decided you really want and need to do. Keep in mind that journeys are not without their hills and valleys and challenges and that, in the words of noted American essayist, John Burroughs, "For anything worth having, one must pay the price; and the price is always work, patience, love, and self-sacrifice."

Accessing Labour Market Information

Fortunately, people today have access to volumes of information and knowledge via the Internet. Even if you don't have a computer, chances are you have a friend or family member who has one that you can use. In the event that this isn't the case, most libraries offer computers for research, as do numerous resource centers such as JobGym and Employment Ontario. I encourage you to utilize this valuable tool and do your own research on Labour Market Information (LMI). There are excellent websites that offer all the pertinent information you need to help you make informed decisions about the future.

I will help get you started by suggesting a couple of sites to explore. Human Resources and Development Canada (http://workplace.hrdc-drhc.gc.ca) is one site that I highly endorse for those living in Canada. Another great site I recommend is, "Making Career Sense of Labour Market Information," a site put together and regularly updated by the Canadian Career Development Foundation, in partnership with HRDC and the British Columbia Ministry of Advanced Education. This site has a wealth of information including factors that help shape labour market trends, such as innovations in technology, political and economic conditions, the globalization of trade, social trends, and demographic changes.

Search these and other sites such as Job Futures (http://jobfutures.ca/jobfutures/) and don't forget about more traditional sources like newspapers, libraries, Ontario Works, and HRDC resource centres.

Another interesting resource to which I would like to refer you is the National Occupational Classification (NOC). It is presented by Human Resources and Skills Development Canada and is the nationally accepted reference on occupations in Canada. It organizes over 30,000 job titles into 520 occupational groups, and is used daily to collect and organize occupational statistics and provide labour market information.

For those residing in the United States you can find similar information at sites such as CareerOneStop, which is sponsored by the US Department of Labour, Employment and Training Administration. Another American-based website is the US States Market Information site in Yahoo directory, which highlights job opportunities state to state. These are just a few examples of websites available to you. Take the time to visit these sites and search for others on your own. There is a wealth of information out there that is only a click away.

A Brief Final Note

The fact that labour market information exists at all reinforces my own decision to stick with career counselling. Although I have sometimes taken a brief hiatus from the job along the way, I came back to it because I have always loved it, knew that I was good at it, and was aware of the continuing need for employment counselling. It is a career that has sustained me, not only financially, but more importantly, emotionally.

The shifting trends that affect occupational availability mean that there will always be people in need of my services, and it is my duty not to just find employment for people but to teach them how to find the right jobs for themselves.

chapter 4

DO I HAVE THE SKILLS AND REQUIREMENTS?

Knowing If You Have What It Takes To Fulfill Your Career Choice

Once you have finalized a decision on what occupational field you plan to pursue and have ascertained that it is a field that is indeed supported by the labour market, the next important area you must address is whether or not you have the proper skills and requirements needed to enter that career.

Education

There was a time long ago when a high school diploma was not necessarily needed to obtain employment. Many people left school because they couldn't handle it or because they were needed at home. They were still able to find jobs in manufacturing plants where they were simply trained to do a specific job. But nowadays, it is essential to have that diploma. So if you have not completed your high school education, I highly recommend that you concentrate on returning to school and earning that diploma. For the majority of jobs out there today, a high school diploma is the minimum requirement you will need. Suffice it to say, your chances of entering a college or university program are nil without this achievement on your resume.

Education has become a vital part of our society and is an important fact to consider when you have decided on a career choice. Research your chosen career field and discover what diplomas or certificates are required to enter it. The National Occupational Classification (NOC) that I mentioned earlier in Chapter 3 is a good resource for finding out this information. You can even access what schools offer certain programs at this site. Job postings will usually list any educational and other requirements needed.

Other factors you must consider with regards to education are how long your program will take and what the cost will be. Are you in a position to take on these issues? Keep in mind that there is always financial assistance offered by the government to those who apply and meet the requirements. Programs such as Second Career Ontario offer funding to help cover tuition and living costs for those who want to train for a new career and are eligible.

Training

Wikipedia defines training as "a term that refers to the acquisition of knowledge, skills, and competencies as a result of teaching of vocational or practical skills and knowledge that relate to specific useful competencies. It forms the core of apprenticeships and provides the backbone of content at institutes of technology."

Many occupations will require certain training certificates before one can apply for a position. For instance, anyone hoping to enter the health care field will be required to already have certification in standard first aid and CPR before being accepted into a related program.

Some jobs, such as electrician, will require you to have a certain amount of training in a specific field prior to being accepted as an apprentice.

It is also important to note that most occupations will require you to develop beyond your initial qualifications through on-going training as it is essential to maintaining, upgrading, and updating skills throughout your career. Again, it is important to research the career of your choice to discover what kind of training is required before being hired for a job, and to learn what kind of training, if any, will be expected of you after you have secured employment.

Experience

"Experience is the teacher of all things." Even Julius Caesar, back in the time before Christ's birth, recognized the importance of experience. Think about times in your life when you have been taught something. It is one thing to be told how to do it, but you don't really experience what you have been instructed to do until you have actually done it yourself.

Experience is a valuable tool to have, not just in work, but of course, in life in general. Hands-on training, where students get to practice what they have learned before they enter the workforce, is common in today's educational system, and for good reason. Imagine if we lived in a world where paramedic students spent all of their time in the classroom and gained no field experience prior to graduation.

It is not uncommon to see job postings that request that applicants have a minimum amount of related experience, and of course, experience speaks volumes when you are applying for a job and there is a lot of competition.

If you are interested in a job that requires more experience than you possess, there are ways of overcoming this shortfall. One of the best methods is to seek out experience through volunteering. Recruiters will be impressed with your effort at acquiring the needed experience and it will better prepare you for the job at hand if you are hired.

Licences and Tickets

Some occupations will expect you to possess certain licences or tickets before legally being allowed to work in that job. These are known as regulatory occupations. For example, people who are interested in employment in the welding trade are required to have tickets that demonstrate that they are proficient in various types of welding procedures. Real estate agents will have to pass courses and receive a licence before they can legally engage in selling houses and property.

As always, it is up to you to thoroughly research the occupation you've chosen to follow, to learn if a licence or ticket is required of you. Again, NOC is an excellent site where you can find this information. Also, most regulatory bodies and apprenticeship authorities have their own websites that provide information on licensing, eligibility requirements, etc. You will discover that regulations differ from province to province, or state to state, and though you may be legally allowed to work in one, your licence may not be accepted in another.

Equipment/Tools

Some companies may expect you to have your own equipment and tools. Today's up and down economy has resulted in this being the case. When considering applying for a position that uses certain tools and equipment, you will need to inquire about what you are expected to bring to the job. You can contact companies directly or speak with someone you may know that is already working in that occupation.

Don't forget that certain clothing requirements may exist in some jobs as well. This may range from something as simple as appropriate apparel, say, if you are seeking a sales position where you will be expected to look professional when dealing with the public, to basic construction needs such as hard hat, safety boots, gloves, and safety eyewear. You will need to know what is required.

Skills

A skill is the ability to do something proficiently, made possible by a person's knowledge, practice, and aptitude. Skills can often be divided into domain-general and domain-specific skills. In the work domain, specific or technical skills would be useful for only a certain position. General skills are those that employers consider to be critical skills required of the general workforce.

General skills can further be divided into three basic categories or skills profiles that employers are looking for in prospective and current employees; academic skills, personal management skills, and teamwork skills. These skills are considered paramount and are required to get, keep, and progress in a job.

Academic skills are the skills that provide the basic foundation. They are broken down into communication, thinking, and learning. With regards to communication, employers need a person who can understand and speak the language in which business is conducted. The person also needs to write effectively in that language. He or she also needs to be able to listen, to understand and learn, as well as to read, comprehend, and use written materials, including charts, graphs and displays.

People must be able to think critically and act logically to evaluate situations, solve problems, and make decisions. They need to understand and solve problems involving mathematics and use the results. Employers will expect them to use technology, instruments, books, and information systems effectively, and to access and apply specialized knowledge from various fields (e.g. skilled trades, technology, physical sciences, arts and social sciences).

When it comes to learning, you will be expected to know how to learn and to continue to learn throughout your career and life. This is essential for maintaining and progressing in your occupation and for adapting to the ever-changing workplace.

Personal management skills are the combinations of skills, attitudes, and behaviours required to get, keep, and progress on a job. Imperative within this profile are positive attitudes and behaviours. Employers seek individuals who can demonstrate self-esteem and confidence and who possess honesty, integrity, and personal ethics.

Teamwork skills are those needed to work effectively with others to achieve the best results on a job. Teamwork skills involve negotiation ability (the ability to pull together with others and refocus on the new common goal), interpersonal skills (abilities that help you cope with the behaviour of others, structure social interaction, share responsibilities and interact more easily with others), and group effectiveness (participative decision-making and problem solving).

Do you have the basic skills that employers are looking for? Try the following assessment exercise to get a better idea.

Identifying Your Skills

Personal Management Skills

1. I take on projects with confidence and know I can do a good job.

   a) Always____
   b) Sometimes____
   c) Never____

2. I tell the truth at work no matter what the consequences are.

   a) Sometimes____
   b) Most of the time____
   c) Never____

3. I volunteer for training and look for opportunities to learn new things.

   a) Always____
   b) Only if it interests me____
   c) Never____

4. I find it difficult to continue with tasks at home and at work, when problems arise.

   a) Most of the time____
   b) Sometimes____
   c) Never____

5. I look for challenges at work and in my spare time.

   a) Most of the time____
   b) Mainly at work____
   c) Mainly in my spare time____

6. I like to set goals and objectives for myself.

   a) Never, it scares me____
   b) Always; it helps me measure my success____
   c) I only do it at work____

7. People tell me I am well organized.

   a) Most of the time____
   b) Sometimes____
   c) Never____

8. I get upset when things change.

   a) Always____
   b) Sometimes____
   c) Never____

9. I like it when people do things differently than I do.

   a) Usually – I learn from them____
   b) Never – they don't do it properly____
   c) It depends____

10. Do you like to think up new and better ways to get your work done?

    a) I don't get paid for that____
    b) Sometimes____
    c) Always; it keeps life interesting and improves my productivity____

What's your score?

(This score sheet can be used for all three quizzes.)

	PERSONAL MANAGEMENT SKILLS	TEAMWORK SKILLS	ACADEMIC SKILLS
1.	a-5 b-3 c-0	1. a-3 b-0 c-5	1. a-3 b-3 c-5
2.	a-3 b-5 c-0	2. a-3 b-5 c-0	2. a-3 b-0 c-5
3.	a-5 b-3 c-0	3. a-0 b-3 c-5	3. a-3 b-5 c-0
4.	a-0 b-3 c-5	4. a-5 b-3 c-0	4. a-5 b-0 c-3
5.	a-5 b-3 c-2	5. a-0 b-5 c-3	5. a-3 b-0 c-5
6.	a-0 b-5 c-3	6. a-5 b-3 c-0	6. a-5 b-3 c-0
7.	a-5 b-3 c-0	7. a-5 b-3 c-0	7. a-0 b-5 c-3
8.	a-0 b-3 c-5	8. a-3 b-0 c-5	8. a-5 b-0 c-3
9.	a-5 b-0 c-3	9. a-3 b-5 c-0	9. a-3 b-0 c-5
10.	a-0 b-3 c-5	10. a-5 b-0 c-3	10. a-5 b-3 c-0
	Total:	Total:	Total:

What's your score?

If you have scored 40 or more: You have good personal management skills that should be highlighted on your resume. Being an excellent organizer or coming up with new and creative ideas are skills that possible employers should know about. A positive attitude, determination to get the job done, and a willingness to learn are all things that could help you impress an employer in an interview situation. You should be able to give examples to the interviewer to demonstrate your abilities in this area.

If you have scored between 25 and 40: You're halfway there! While you have some personal management skills, others need work. Read the next paragraph to get ideas on how to improve in this area. Look for opportunities to practice them.

If you have scored less than 25: Get organized! A course on organizational skills would be helpful to you. In order to get ahead in life and on the job you need to set personal goals. Sit down and decide where you want to be in five years from now. It can be as simple as having a job or as ambitious as having your own business. Believe in yourself! If you know you can do the job, others will too. Employers are looking for people with positive outlooks on the job, who do not give up easily, and who can organize their work and their day-to-day lives.

No matter what your score be open to new challenges! The work place is always changing and you have to keep pace with it. You can expect any job you do to involve many changes over time and you will probably have several jobs over the course of your lifetime. You may have to take on new tasks or learn new ways of doing things. Think of these challenges as opportunities – the more flexible you are, the better your chances for success in a changing work place. Learning new skills is a positive step forward. An employee who wants to learn is a valuable asset to any company.

Teamwork Skills

1. On the job, I make an effort to understand and contribute to the goals of the team.

　　a) Sometimes____ b) Never____ c) Always____

2. Working in a group...

   a) makes me nervous____ b) helps me to get the job done____
   c) takes too much time____

3. When you work with a group, do you find it hard when you can't do things your own way?

   a) Always____ b) Sometimes____ c) Never____

4. Can you plan and make decisions with others?

   a) Most of the time____ b) Sometimes____ c) Not usually____

5. Do you respect the thoughts and opinions of others?

   a) It depends____ b) Always____ c) Usually____

6. Do you mind when other people offer their ideas of how to solve a problem or take on a task?

   a) No, I like it____ b) If I know them____ c) Never____

7. Are you comfortable asking others for help and advice?

   a) Most of the time____ b) If I know them____ c) Never____

8. Would you like to take charge of a group of people if it is working on something you know a lot about?

   a) I'd rather not but I will____ b) I couldn't____ c) Absolutely____

9. Do you think others see you as someone they can turn to for help or advice?

   a) I don't know____ b) Yes____ c) No____

10. If I had a problem on the job and I knew a co-worker had the answer, I would ask him or her for help.

   Always____ b) Never____ c) Sometimes____

What's your score?

If you have scored 40 or more: You are a good team player! Working well with others is a very important skill to have. It means that you understand and appreciate the differences between team members to the best advantage. Once in a while, you may even need to lead a team project. Don't be afraid to take charge when appropriate. Those who feel comfortable working both alone and in a group are valuable assets to their organizations. Make sure you let potential employers know that you are a team player. Include it on your resume by describing some team activity in which you worked successfully.

If you have scored between 25 and 40: You're a team player some of the time. There are obviously instances when you work well in a group and that's great! However, you could use a few tips in this area so read on.

If you have scored less than 25: Doing things on your own is something you may be used to, but there are times when 'two heads are better than one.' You have to learn how to work well with others. Being able to consider the ideas and approaches of co-workers, even if they are different from your own, will help you to work well in a group and get things done. Listen to what other people have to say. You may be surprised at some of the good ideas they have. Offer to help them. If you have never had to work with others, now is a good time to start. Find a neighbourhood club or volunteer organization and join in their activities.

Academic Skills

1. Can you understand and speak English and/or French?

    a) English____ b) French____ c) Both____

2. I am told that I am a good listener.

    a) Sometimes____ b) Never____ c) Often____

3. Do you enjoy reading?

    a) I read when I have to____ b) I love reading____ c) I don't like reading____

4. Can you read, understand, and use written material? (For example, reading a map or following a recipe or a set of instructions to assemble a toy or piece of furniture.)

    a) Yes____ b) No____ c) It depends

5. Do you write well in English and/or French? (For example, letters to friends, memos, instructions or lists.)

    a) It depends____ b) Writing is a challenge____ c) Yes, always____

6. Do you like making decisions?

    a) Most of the time____ b) Sometimes____ c) I find it difficult____

7. Do people come to you to help them solve problems at work or at home?

    a) Never____ b) All the time____ c) Sometimes____

8. Can you solve problems that require basic math skills? (For example, balancing a cheque book, making change or working with measurements.)

   a) No problem____ b) Math scares me____ c) I can with effort

9. Can you use technology like computers, email, Internet, and Blackberry?

   a) I'm trying to learn____ b) Never used____
   c) I use them all the time____

10. Do you have special knowledge or training that you could use at work?

    a) A trade, degree or college diploma____
    b) Computer skills____ c) No special training____

What's your score?

If you have scored more 30 or more: You have skills and talents that are valued by employers. Remember, however, that the work place is constantly changing. A job you do or a skill you have now may need to be upgraded tomorrow or it may be eliminated. The key to employment success is education. Set goals for yourself based on continuing learning. No matter what level of education or what specific trade you have, think of improving it. Some employers and organizations will even help pay for courses taken by their employees. Never stop learning! The more you know, the better your chances of finding and keeping a job. Employers are looking for people who are adaptable and have several skills.

If you have scored less than 30: Your academic skills may need a tune-up! The single most important factor that an employer looks at when hiring, is the level of education and technical skills. If you never finished high school, try to do it now. There are evening and correspondence courses you can take that don't have to interfere too much with your everyday activities. Two-thirds of jobs created in the future will require at least high school graduation.

If you have a high school diploma but no specific employment skills, look into a training program at a local community college. Talk to the counsellors at these schools. Find out what skills are in demand in your area and apply for a course to get them. There are also adult night courses available at many high schools.

If you have a specific trade, talk to the counsellors at the local community college. Find out if there are new skills being taught in your trade since you graduated. If so, take time to upgrade.

If you have a college diploma or a degree in the arts, it's time to supplement it. Employers need people who have specific skills, like being able to work with computers or having more than one language. Find out what skills are most in demand right now and make sure you get them.

No matter what your score: Learn more by doing. A lot of employers like to hire people with experience. If you don't have any, get it. There are hundreds of volunteer organizations that could use your help. Offer your services and get the experience you need to impress future employers.

Transferable Skills

Transferable skill is a term you should become familiar with and understand. Transferable or functional skills are skills you've attained from having done various jobs, volunteering, hobbies, sports, or other life experiences. These skills can be used from one occupation or job to another.

Your functional skills can relate to things, people, and data or information. Here are some example lists of transferable skills:

Dealing with things:

» Using hands or fingers – feeling, gathering, separating, sorting, applying, pressing, etc.
» Having finger dexterity – keyboarding, sense of touch, playing, dealing, etc.
» Eye-Hand co-ordination – balancing, juggling, drawing, etc.
» Motor/physical co-ordination of body – raising, lifting, carrying, pushing, pulling, moving, etc.
» Craft, model, mould, sculpt, etc.
» Finish/refinish, renovate
» Repair, fix, maintain, clean, adjust
» Set up, assemble
» Operate, control, drive
» Oversee, tend, mind, feed, monitor, etc.
» Break down, disassemble, salvage
» Analyze, trouble-shoot
» Construct, build
» Handle, expedite, deliver, etc.
» Make, produce, manufacture

Dealing with people:

» Take instructions, serve, help
» Communicate orally – question, answer, reply, inform, sign, exchange information
» Communicate in writing, author
» Instruct, teach, train, facilitate
» Advise, coach, counsel, mentor
» Diagnose, treat, heal
» Consult, network, collaborate
» Assess, evaluate, monitor
» Persuade, convince, sell
» Motivate, empower, encourage
» Advocate, represent

- » Demonstrate, model, present
- » Perform, entertain, act
- » Lead, manage, direct
- » Negotiate, reconcile, mediate, etc.
- » Advise, recommend, decide
- » Organize, co-ordinate, stage, control
- » Screen, select, recruit
- » Supervise, delegate

Dealing with data/information

- » Research, investigate, determine, etc.
- » Survey, collect, compile, retrieve
- » Observe, perceive, verify, check
- » Interview, inquire, ask (for information)
- » Study, examine, observe
- » Manage, administer, control
- » Invent, create, design (ideas)
- » Analyze, pull apart, scrutinize, compare
- » Synthesize, pull together, link
- » Account, reconcile, calculate, estimate (numbers)
- » Organize, classify, prioritize, etc.
- » Apply, implement, introduce, etc.
- » Plan, lay out, sequence, streamline
- » Adapt, adjust
- » Forecast, estimate, budget, anticipate
- » Report, summarize, record
- » Publicize, advertise, market
- » Problem-solve, decide
- » Screen, select, extract, edit
- » Critique, evaluate, assess, decide, recommend, etc.
- » Manage, administer

The following is an example list of personality/self-management/adaptive skills:

» Efficient, effective
» Imaginative, creative, resourceful, innovative
» Accurate, precise, thorough
» Perceptive, alert, observant
» Enthusiastic, keen
» Sensitive, empathetic, understanding
» Fair, responsive, decisive
» Tactful, diplomatic, discreet
» Competitive, assertive, aggressive
» Co-operate, team player
» Initiative, self-directed, change agent, leader
» Articulate, clear, well spoken
» Entrepreneurial
» Results/Goal oriented
» Sense of humour
» Committed, loyal, dependable
» Responsible, accountable, trustworthy
» Adaptable, flexible
» Independent
» Optimistic, positive

Seven Experiences (Adapted from Kate Wendleton's book *Through the Brick Wall*[3])

Here is another little exercise I like to conduct in my workshops that you will find helpful in identifying and clarifying your skills and learning how to adapt them in your job search. Select seven experiences from your life that you enjoyed. They do not have to be work-oriented.

---

[3] Wendleton, Kate. *Through the Brick Wall: How to Job-Hunt in a Tight Market.* Toronto. Random House. 1992. Print

You can choose from past work (paid or volunteer), education or training, hobbies, a special project or event, or a family-related situation.

List these experiences and then write a short paragraph for each one. Identify any special knowledge, credentials, or technical expertise you have that relates to each experience. Now review the previous example lists dealing with Transferable/Functional skills and Personality/Self management/Adaptive skills. You may interpret the meaning of the skills any way you wish. If you used this skill in an experience, then make a single check mark. If you used the skill and excelled at it, make a double check mark. Feel free to add any skills you may have that are not listed here.

After reviewing the lists, you can identify any trends or expertise. Ask yourself: Do I wish to continue to use these skills in my next job or career? Summarize and write down your key skills. Finally, review the lists again. Are there any skills you wish to develop? Summarize and write these down as well.

I am sure that by completing this exercise, you will gain a better understanding of your skills and how these can be used to aid you in your career search.

A Quick Note about My Own Experiences

I like to end each chapter with a personal story or experience that relates to the content. I want you all to know that I am not just preaching at or teaching you, but that I have had my share of experiences and can relate to all of this.

I guess the best example of how skills and requirements have worked for me with my own employment journey, would be the skills I learned and developed as an early childhood educator and how these skills helped me with my transition from working with 'wee' ones to teaching and guiding adults.

As a career counsellor, I have been able to use what I learned in my years of working in daycares and with children, and to adapt that knowledge and experience to working with adults. Whether we are five years old or fifty years old, we are still human beings. We develop in our youth and continue to grow and learn throughout life. The only difference is that as adults we may face more challenges because of the baggage we accumulate along the way.

As I have stated throughout the book, my education in the field of employment counselling has been ongoing and continues today. My training has given me certification in many aspects of career counselling, including as a Career Development Facilitator, and in such recognized assessment tools such as Myers Briggs Type Indicator®, True Colours-Level I and II, and Emotional Intelligence.

These courses have helped me excel in teaching unemployed clients as well as people looking to make a career change. My education has helped me in working closely with and mentoring supervisors, managers, human resources specialists, and other career counsellors.

Never stop exploring. Never stop learning. Never give up on your dreams!

chapter 5

EMPOWERING BELIEFS?

Coping with change
And taking control of your future

"He who rejects change is the architect of decay. The only institution which rejects progress is the cemetery."

British Prime Minister Harold Wilson

Understanding Change

Many centuries ago, the Greek philosopher Heraclitus said, "The only constant is change." Like it or not, change has been occurring since the dawn of time. Therefore, it is important to be able to recognize change and to learn how to deal with it, or even use it to our benefit. Resisting change is not only futile but can also be counterproductive.

Take some time to think about changes that have happened over the past decades and how these shifts have affected the world of work. Globalization, recession, and free trade, just to name a few, have had distinct impacts on the job force. The traditional path of simply getting a good education, finding a job, and remaining in that occupation for twenty or thirty years has become a thing of the past.

Most people will experience several occupational changes in their lifetime and students entering a university program can expect that the profession for which they are studying may undergo significant alterations before they graduate. No wonder stress levels have increased considerably in today's society.

Fortunately, human beings are resilient and have a history of adapting to their changing world. The fact that civilization has survived to this point is testament of that. Surviving in the modern-day workforce is also dependant on adapting to change and making smart decisions that allow positive transitions.

The Stages of Change

When people are suddenly thrust into a position of unemployment, whether because of their own decisions or circumstances beyond their control, a range of emotional patterns will be experienced. Dealing with job loss is not much dissimilar from how people react to the loss of a loved one or a diagnosis of a terminal illness. I can personally attest to this, having lost my mother to cancer.

In 1969, Elisabeth Kubler-Ross documented the stages of grief and loss in her ground-breaking book, *On Death and Dying*[4]. Losing a job can be compared to a death since it involves the loss of income, routine, and role identity as well as the fear of facing an uncertain future. Kubler-Ross's model describes five different stages – denial, anger, bargaining, depression, and finally, acceptance. We will look at these phases and consider how they relate to the changes that are experienced when one is faced with job loss and the uncertainties that accompany it.

---

[4] Kubler-Ross, Elizabeth. *On Death and Dying*. New York, Scribner. 1969. Print

Denial

The first stage is a psychological defence mechanism that attempts to protect the individual from experiencing the full brunt of a loss in the beginning. A person may feel shock or numbness and may make statements such as "this can't be happening," or "everything is going to be okay." This stage is usually a brief period.

After my time with HRDC I became the chairperson for a labour force adjustment group and was involved with workers from a local manufacturing company who were left in limbo for nine months, wondering what was happening with the company. Although it was well known to us that this organization was finished and would not be starting up again, workers keeping an eye on the site would see activity and movement. The ripple effect that followed was indicative of the denial stage. Word spread fast that just maybe the plant was going to reopen and people would be getting back to work. In reality, the activity they witnessed was actually connected to the land being surveyed for sale and things being moved. Even months of unemployment had failed to remove the workers' belief that everything was ok and their jobs were safe. They were stuck in the denial stage and because of that had been unable to move on and make plans for their future. Meanwhile the 'higher-ups', having seen the writing on the wall some time ago, were long gone.

Anger

When people finally realize that their situations are a reality and move away from denial, they will usually experience anger. This is a time where they may project feelings of resentment towards the company, the management, or even coworkers who may still be working. They will look for someone or something to blame. Keep in mind that not all will have the same response. Some may feel a sense of relief in becoming unemployed because they were unhappy with their jobs. However, these people may just be deluding themselves when, in actuality, they are in fear of the change and the uncertain future that comes with it. It is important to note that anger, as well as each other stage, is not only natural but necessary in the healing process. It is okay to be angry and important to express your feelings in order to move on to the next phase. The sooner you accept the feelings and deal with them, the sooner you will move on and reach a point where positive growth begins. Sharing your emotions is very helpful, whether it be with family, friends, or people you meet who are in the same situation. Having a support system is crucial.

Bargaining

Facing bad news will often lead people to negotiate or bargain to lessen the pain of loss. Once a person has dealt with and progressed away from anger, they will typically enter this phase. Someone given news of impending death might barter with God, in such a way as, "I'll go to church more often," or "I'll be a better person if you just make this better or give me more time to see my children grow up," etc. Individuals who find themselves out of work might offer to work more hours or even take pay cuts in order to keep their jobs. They might think, "If only I'd worked harder or been a better employee, this might not have happened to me." Again, this is a mechanism by which the individual is attempting to resist the inevitable.

Depression

Inevitably, people who suffer the death of a loved one or who are informed that they themselves are dying will be faced with a period of depression. They may become reclusive and antisocial. Their sadness might lead them to thoughts of, "Why should I bother with anything when I'm just going to die anyway?" or "How do I go on without my loved one?" Typically, those who suffer a change in their employment situation will experience very similar feelings. They may dwell on the negatives and find themselves discouraged and with a low energy level. Sleeping and eating habits might become altered. This is an important part of the mourning process as it forces us to think seriously about what has transpired and how it affects our lives. Thankfully, it is also a time when people will start to reflect on the future, a step that already has them moving forward into the next stage.

Acceptance

This final stage has also been defined as "the end of the dying struggle." This is the phase where a person finally reaches an understanding of the situation and comes to terms with it. A sense of doom is replaced with a sense of peace.

Accepting the inevitable, a person will tell themselves, "I can't change this so I might as well prepare for it." They will start to feel better and actually begin considering how they might turn this change into an opportunity. They will look to the future and make plans; exploring possibilities and becoming more proactive.

The Change Curve

Kubler-Ross eventually broadened the application of these stages to include any major form of personal loss such as employment, income, or freedom. She went on to state that not everyone will cycle through the stages in a specific order and that some may experience the same phase multiple times or get stuck in a specific stage, unable to move on. Only when we are able to manage each stage can we truly move forward and begin setting goals for the future. If people attempt to move on but are still locked in a stage where their emotions are negative and hindering them, the results will not be very successful. As the ancient Greek playwright Euripides once said, "Do not plan for ventures before finishing what's at hand."

For example, imagine that you are a human resources manager in charge of hiring people for a company. Now imagine you are interviewing someone who is obviously harbouring feelings of anger or depression. This person might have all the right qualifications and loads of experience but if his or her demeanour is obviously down, you are not likely to hire that person over someone with the same qualifications, but who conducts the interview with confidence and an upbeat attitude.

Take a look at the change curve graph.

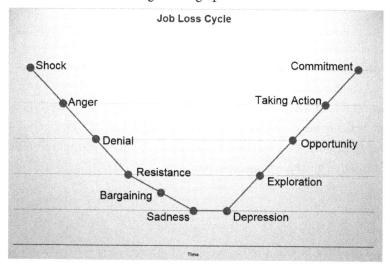

It is a simple tool that further illustrates the sequence of events a person can expect to experience when dealing with job loss. Notice that deny and resist are associated with the past. Although, as stated previously, it is important to live through these emotions, it is also imperative to deal with them and move to the other side of the chart, in order to have any hope of turning change into a positive situation of growth. Those who fail to elevate themselves to the other side of the chart are sure to experience extremely negative results. Unfortunately, these are the people who never return to the job force and are dependent on government assistance for the remainder of their lives, or who may even join the ranks of the homeless.

The reasons for this can be many. On top of having the psychological effects associated with job loss, such as anger, sadness, and depression and not being able to manage them, some are also hindered by other serious problems such as chemical dependencies or marital difficulties. Unless these issues are addressed, the chances of becoming ready to explore future options in a positive manner are slim.

Fortunately, most people are resilient and with the proper knowledge, support, and direction are able to progress to the more positive, right side of the graph where exploration and commitment exist. They can start to analyze and examine opportunities available to them and eventually commit to employment goals.

Resistance to change is quite understandable because we are creatures of habit and become content with our existing conditions even if we really aren't happy. We all have our comfort zones. "Our dilemma is that we hate change and love it at the same time; what we really want is for things to remain the same but get better" (Sydney J. Harris, Chicago Daily News journalist and author).

Of course, for things to get better we must experience change even though we may fear the unknowns associated with it. Everything we do in life is motivated by either faith or fear. If we let fear dictate our lives we can never move forward. However, if we have faith that any situation can be turned into a good thing and actually envision it in our minds, the chances for success are obviously greater.

I am sure that most of you are familiar with the concept of self-fulfilling prophecy. When people think in negative ways they tend to act in ways that will not get them what they want: What you think is what you get. This is an especially damaging way of thinking during change because it causes people not to try new ways or take risks.

You may not accept it but I can vouch for it in my own personal experience. When I was going through a period of tribulation it was difficult not to expect more bad things to happen and more times than not, this turned out to be the case. Only when I took control of the negative situations and started to visualize and focus on the possibility of positive things happening did these scenarios start to actually appear.

Limiting Beliefs vs. Empowering Beliefs

The first step in changing your beliefs is to take a look at what you have been telling yourself about change. Limiting beliefs are just that: beliefs that limit your abilities. Take some time to think about limiting beliefs you may have about yourself, your work environment, and the changes you are experiencing. It is helpful to even list these on paper so you can visualize them more easily. Now review this list. Ask yourself how these limiting beliefs can be replaced with empowering beliefs.

If you say, "I can't do this," an empowering belief would be, "I can learn how to do this." Through positive affirmative beliefs, you will begin to feel more powerful and in control of your life. If you really believe that you can't do something, then you will not be able to do it. Don't underestimate the power of your own mind. Influences by external forces can hinder and even block you from reaching goals if you are unable to look past them and look inside yourself for the answers to taking control of your own life.

Also keep in mind that if you are surrounded by negative people, their influence will have a negative affect on you as well. You know those days where you start off feeling great and then encounter a negative person. I liken it to pulling up in a Cadillac and before you know it, you're driving away in an old, beat-up Chevette. You're not sure how it happened but somehow that person is now driving away in the Caddy, waving goodbye. These people are emotional vampires and my advice to you is that when you see the 'Chevettes' just keep on driving and don't even wave. It is important to stay focused on the positives if you are to have any hope for success in your life.

As I've mentioned, before I became involved in career counselling I went to school for and became an early childhood educator. It was a job I thoroughly enjoyed because I love children and the opportunities that come with teaching and helping to mould such young, developing minds. I was even fortunate enough to open and run my own daycare for a time. However, it seems that people will pay more money to have their pets cared for than they will to ensure proper education for their little ones. Though the occupation had many benefits, the financial rewards were far below what I needed to provide myself and my son with the kind of lifestyle I wanted for us, and that is why I eventually moved onto different employment.

During my time in this job, however, I learned some very valuable lessons that I have carried through life and have used in my present-day occupation of guiding adults in their quest for employment satisfaction. One of the things I found is that if someone is told no over and over or "you can't do that," a person will develop a negative sense of himself or herself. I remember one case where a little boy in our class was trying to cut a pencil in half with a pair of scissors.

This was not appropriate so naturally I tried to get him to stop by telling him, "No, you shouldn't do that," "Stop doing that," "That's not right," etc. If any of you have children you'll understand what I mean. I went to my administrator at the time for guidance with this situation and when I asked her advice she simply said, "How about telling him scissors are for cutting paper."

Well not only was that elementary but it was also a more positive approach to correcting the situation. Imagine that little Johnny hears, "No, you can't do that," all day long. He's sure to go home thinking he can't do anything right and we all know what kind of impact that will have on his personality. Adults are no different in that if we are constantly told no, it will have a damaging effect on our egos and our confidence factor. Therefore it is important when dealing with change to maintain that positive attitude and stay clear of the negative, defeatist influences.

Remember that you have the power to change and to adapt to change. Contrary to the popular old adage – you CAN teach old dogs new tricks!

The Personal Transition Work Sheet[5]

Some people are ready for change and others are not. Some live in such a way that transition is a minor disruption, while others have lives that are brought to a standstill by transitions. How prepared are you? The following is an exercise that I use in my workshops to help clients better understand themselves and how ready or not they are to deal with changes.

Complete the assessment by putting numbers
in the spaces to the left of the item.

4 = Yes, definitely
3 = Somewhat
2 = Not very much
1 = Not at all

____1. Do I believe that I have really come to terms with the fact that today's change is continuous and that stability can only be achieved by means of constant, little changes?

____2. Do I view change as both a stressor and an opportunity?

____3. Am I developing a pretty effective early-warning system to spot and address changes that are emerging in my life and career?

____4. When I spot change on the horizon, am I responding by undertaking a 'learning project' to prepare myself to deal with it effectively?

____5. Am I actively seeking all the information I can get about my present change – what it means for me and what I can do about it?

---

[5] Adapted from William Bridges & Associates, 1992

____6. Do I understand that change causes transition and that transition must start by losing or leaving behind the old way and least some small aspect of my old identity?

____7. Do I truly understand what is currently ending for me and that it is time for me to let go?

____8. Am I responding to such endings and losses by developing an action plan?

____9. Have I found ways in my life to mark the endings and even ceremonialize the relinquishment process I am going through?

____10. Do I understand and can I accept the necessity of going through 'mourning' in dealing with my loss(es)?

____11. Have I found symbolic 'pieces of the past' to take along with me?

____12. Am I sorting through my situation, discovering the continuities in my life, and making plans to strengthen them?

____13. Have I created temporary systems to provide me with the sources to control, understanding, support, and purpose during this time?

____14. Do I have someone with whom I can share whatever I am feeling and thinking about my present situation?

____15. Am I using this time as an opportunity to step back and take stock of who I am and how I am living?

____16. Am I rethinking what I want to become and accomplish before my life is over?

____17. Am I using all that I know about creativity and innovation to capitalize on the 'blank slate' provided by the time period?

____18. Specifically, am I looking at who I really am today, what I really want out of my life and what I do best?

___19. Am I using this data as the raw material for a new personal vision of the future?

___20. Am I also looking at the organization I work for, the community I live in, and people like me, as resources for whatever this self-assessment process produces?

___21. Am I putting together a personal action plan to define my objectives and to realize them?

___22. While recognizing the opportunities in my situation, do I also acknowledge it as a time of high stress and do I have a personal stress management plan to handle it?

___23. Stepping back from the immediate demands of the situation, can I see it as a time of meaning and personal significance for me… as a time with a lesson to teach?

___ Total the number scores and convert them into letter grades.

82 – 92 A
72 – 81 B
62 – 71 C
50 is a 'passing' grade

In light of your score on this self-assessment index, think about what you might do to make your situation more manageable and meaningful.

Decision Making

Now that you are better informed about the importance of change and the affect it has on your life, it is imperative to look at the process of decision-making. You have been making several decisions every day since you were a small child. There are many ways of making decisions and most of us have a method we use, of which we are often not even aware. Since we are constantly faced with change throughout our lives and will have to make important decisions regarding those changes, it only makes sense to delve into decision-making and to discover how we make everyday decisions.

Wikipedia says that, "Decision making can be regarded as the cognitive (mental) process resulting in the selection of a course of action among several alternatives. Every decision-making process produces a final choice. The output can be an action or an opinion of choice."

Proper decision making is crucial when we are trying to make our lives better, especially when we are in search of that occupation that will meet all of our needs and desires. Here are eight typical ways that people make decisions:

1. The hopeful method: Picking the 'nicest' choice and crossing your fingers, hoping it works out right.

2. The safe method: Picking the 'safest' choice, the one involving the least amount of risk.

3. The 'go for it' method: Deciding without thinking about it first – not looking before you leap.

4. The 'whatever you say' method: Letting someone else decide for you – giving up control.

5. The over-analyzing method: Taking apart every option and analyzing it to death until you are more confused than when you began.

6. The feeling method: Choosing the path that feels right – trusting your gut-level feelings and instincts.

7. The non-deciding method: Delaying or ignoring the situation until there is no decision to be made.

8. The planning method: Considering all the choices and evaluating them with your end goal in mind.

We have all used each of these methods at various times throughout our lives and in different situations. Take a moment to reflect on a past decision you made in your life where the result was regrettable, and then think of one where the outcome was more satisfactory. Now, reviewing the eight methods, consider which one you probably used in each decision.

Decision making can often be hard because it can involve conflict and dissatisfaction. Avoiding decisions may seem the easiest route to take sometimes, but the results will be beyond your control. In the words of the late Will Rogers, "Even if you are on the right track, you will get run over if you just sit there." The only true way to take control of your time, your success, your life, and your future is by making your own decisions and accepting the consequences.

> The following is a list of decision-making techniques you may find helpful, not only as they relate to your search for the perfect job fit but also to your life in general.

1. Identify the purpose of your decision. What exactly is the problem to be solved and why it should be solved?
2. Gather information. What factors does the problem involve?
3. Identify the principles to judge the alternatives. What standards and judgement criteria should the solution meet?
4. Brainstorm and list different possible choices. Generate ideas for possible solutions.
5. Evaluate each choice in terms of its consequences. Use your standards and judgement criteria to determine the pros and cons of each alternative.
6. Determine the best alternative. This will be much easier after you have gone through the previous steps.

7. Put the decision into action. Transform your decision into a specific plan of action steps. Execute your plan.

8. Evaluate the outcome of your decision and action steps. What lessons can be be learned? This is an important step for further development of decision-making skills and judgement.

In Chapter 2, I mentioned the Myers Briggs Type Indicator® and how it related to getting a better understanding of ourselves and others. I refer to it here again because of the third scale of the MBTI® and how it pertains to decision making. I think it is beneficial to remind you to reflect on what kind of decision maker you are and whether or not this works for you. Are you a Thinker-Decider who prefers to organize and structure information in a logical, objective way, or are you the Feeling-Decider who organizes and structures information to decide in a personal, value-oriented way?

Remember that decisions you make can have lasting and crucial consequences in life. Many people experience a roller coaster-type ride when it comes to employment because of the decisions and choices they have made along the way. The only way you will discover the right occupation for you is to take control of your life by recognizing and coping with change, and then making the appropriate decisions to deal with the changes and forge on to the future.

My Own Story – The Best Decisions of My Life

I would like to end this chapter by sharing a very personal life story in hopes that it will be an example to all of you of how I have coped with changes in my life and the decisions I made along the way that brought me to this place in my journey. Quite often, when people are going through times of trouble they feel like they are the only one experiencing such times. Remember that you are not alone and that many others actually have it a lot worse. You may feel unfortunate 'because you have no shoes' until you see someone who 'has no feet.'

I grew up in a very dysfunctional household and in my teenage years there were many stresses on the family. Needless to say, I couldn't wait to get out of the house and 'be on my own,' but that opportunity came in the form of an ill-advised marriage. Soon I found myself a struggling single mother, and later entered into another marriage that also failed.

In short, I have been faced with a lot of transitions in my life and it wasn't until I finally made the decision to stop being a victim and take control of my life that I was able to move forward and find peace. Of this decision I am very proud. I took it upon myself to forgive those who had wronged me in my past, and I replaced limiting beliefs and feelings with empowering ones. I chose to be better instead of bitter. Today I can reflect on my past without tears, without sadness, and without anger because I chose to finally face the past head-on and take a proactive approach to assuming control over my future instead of letting others control it for me.

I am in a good place now, happy with my occupation, and happy with my life. You too can have the same results if you truly desire!

chapter 6

DO I KNOW HOW AND WHERE TO LOOK FOR WORK? AM I ABLE TO MAINTAIN A JOB?

Helpful Tips for Job Searching and Important Facts to Consider for Employment Success

If you have thoroughly considered the first three questions, (Do I have clear career goals? Will the labour market support my choice? Do I have the skills and requirements?) and are satisfied and confident with your answers, you are ready to explore the final questions. Knowing how and where to look for work will require you to be very proactive. The more time and energy you spend answering this question, the better your chance at success in securing the employment you desire. Research is crucial at this stage of the journey.

While question-three will challenge you in searching for and acquiring valuable information regarding employment, the final question will challenge you to explore your very life and soul. It is similar to question-one, in that if a sufficient answer cannot be arrived upon, then it makes no sense to continue on your journey until you are satisfied with the answer.

I will give you a brief overview of the questions and some tips to aid you in answering them. I encourage and challenge you to put forth an honest effort in expanding your knowledge about job searching AND in taking a good look around you, a good look inside of you, and a 'good look in the mirror!'

Information Gathering

No doubt the twenty-first century will bring even more complexity to what we know as information. You will need to be ever more capable of envisioning the future, and what you need to learn or do to keep pace with the labour market trends that will affect your career and life.

The challenge that we face is knowing how to use information in career planning. The tremendous source of labour market information, which is available can give us profit and wisdom. To understand information we must define the terminology. Information is the communication of knowledge. It is data (primarily numbers) that has been synthesized and formatted into words. Data is the measurement of an occurrence, event or object; raw materials from which information is derived. For example: The score is 54; the unemployment rate is 5.6%; computer maintenance technicians will grow at a rate of 2.8%; there are 181,000 carpenters in Canada.

An example of information would be: There is currently a balance between the number of applicants and the number of openings for Computer Maintenance Technicians. Future outlook depends on the sales of computer equipment and technological changes. The sales of computer equipment are expected to rise rapidly, but the number of Computer Maintenance Technicians is expected to rise more slowly because of technological advances in the new equipment requiring less maintenance and repair.

Your awareness and exploration of quality labour-market information will greatly contribute toward sound career decision-making and realistic planning. Again, I will make reference to the National

Occupational Classification, an excellent source of labour market information (www.23.hrdc-drhc.gc.ca/)

Other LMI related websites include:

Job Bank (http://www.jobbank.ca)
Jobs, Workers, Training and Careers Cluster (www.jobsetc.ca)
Job Futures (National Edition) (http://jobfutures.ca)
Provincial Job Futures (http://www.input regional information)
Sector Councils (www.councils.org)
Provincial Apprenticeship Websites
Ontario Government Labour Market
Site (www.ontario.ca/labourmarket)

Some websites to explore in the United States:

» U.S. Bureau of Labor Statistics (www.bls.gov/)
» Federal Statistical Agencies (www.bls.gov/blswage.htm)
» Employment Projections Home Page (www.bls.gov/emp/)
» CareerOneStop (www.careeronestop.org/lmi/lmihome.asp)

I encourage you to utilize the Internet to discover the vast amount of career and employment-related information available to you. Not only can it be used in understanding the market and its current and future trends, but it can also be a useful tool when conducting your actual job search.

Researching Specific Jobs

When you have reached the stage where you have set your sights on a specific position, it is important to gather information about not only the job and what it entails, but also about the company or employer where the position exists and the industry it represents. This will give you a better idea of whether the position meets your requirements and goals, and just what is expected of you, should you be hired. As well, being able to demonstrate your knowledge of the company to a recruiter during the interview process will go a long way in impressing them. They will know that you have, "done your homework!"

The following chart will give you an overview of some of the facts you should consider and who and where to go to for the information:

Factor	What to Consider	Who/Where to Search
Job	Duties	NOC book/Job ads
	Work conditions	Counsellors
	Wages/Benefits	Economists
	Hours	Library
	Education/Experience/Training	Associations/Unions
	Environmental conditions	Surveys
	Licences	College/University
	Special clothing/Tools	LMI
	Travel	
	Language reference	
Company	Product/Service	Trade journals
	Reputation	Prospectus
	Age/Size	Stockbrokers
	Diversity	Employees
	Mission statement	Suppliers
	Key personnel	Yellow pages
	Structure	Libraries
	Employee equity	Associations/Unions
	Unionized?	Economic development
	Domestic/Foreign owned	
	Restructuring?	Fortune 500
	How do they hire?	

Industry > Future trends > Suppliers
   > Competition > Library
   > Business cycle > Newspapers > Government regulations/
   Political impact > Business publications
   > Supply/Demand > Stockbrokers
   > International? > Directories
   > Markets > Employer/Employees
   > Sectors in economy > Associations/Unions
   > Salary ranges

Before entering into your search, I believe that you will find it extremely helpful to consider all these factors carefully and actually put your research plan down on paper, complete with appropriate questions. It will make your action plan more organized and solid and help you have a better vision of the overall picture.

As I have stated before and can't stress enough, it is so important to become passionate about your career search and therefore genuinely give it your best attention and effort. Doing so will only increase your possibility for success. It really is up to you to educate yourself in every aspect of the subject.

Cover Letter, Resumes and Interviews

Two of the most basic and common tools in job searching are cover letters and resumes. A cover letter is an introduction letter accompanying your resume. It introduces you and briefly documents your suitability for the position for which you are applying. Recruiters look for cover letters that are thoughtfully constructed and individualized, as they use the letter as a screening tool when considering prospective employees.

Cover Letter

Normally, a cover letter is no longer than one page in length and is divided into four sections: First is the Header, which includes the sender's address and other information as well as the recipient's address. This is followed by a salutation such as, "Dear Human Resources Manager." Next is the Introduction, which briefly states the position you are seeking and should be designed to attract the reader's immediate interest. This section is followed by the Body of the letter. This will highlight material in the resume and explain why you are interested in the position and why you would be an asset to the company. This section will also include your skills, qualifications, and past experience. Special information, such as a date when you would be available to start the job, can be inserted in the body.

The final part of the cover letter is the closing. It is a summary of the letter and an indication of your next intention, such as contacting the employer directly or waiting to hear back from them. The letter concludes with a valediction, such as "sincerely," and a written signature.

You can find out much more about cover letters, including samples and tips on proficient cover-letter writing on the Internet, as well as in libraries and employment resource centres.

Resume

The importance of a well-written resume cannot be overlooked. It can mean the difference between getting a call for an interview or not. Usually, it consists of one to three pages and directs the recruiter's attention to aspects of your background and how they relate directly to the specific position you seek. The resume should be long enough to properly provide concise, adequate, and accurate descriptions of your employment history and your skills. For best results, it should be job specific; that is to say, it should be adapted to suit each individual job application and/or applications aimed at a specific industry.

Most efficient resumes will include keywords that employers look for, as well as liberal use of active verbs, and they should display content in a flattering manner. There are two basic styles of resumes that are commonly used. The Chronological Resume is a style that lists job experiences in a reverse chronological order and generally covers the past ten years. This style is not recommended if you have gaps in your employment history.

The Functional Resume's focus is more on position-specific work experience and skills rather than a simple work history. It is recommended for those who have experienced periods of unemployment whereby gaps exist in their job history. Again, helpful hints on constructing resumes can be found at various sources such as the Internet or a career-counselling organization.

With the advent and progress of the Electronic Information Age, it is important to familiarize yourself with the online resume process. More and more employers and companies are using the Internet in their search for employees. You must choose a file format in which to maintain your resume. Many employers insist on receiving Word Document resumes exclusively, but there are other formats such as PDF.

A lot of today's companies use search machines with regards to screening resumes, so again, the use of keywords can be very important to getting your resume noticed. Many large companies are using electronic resume processing systems so they can more efficiently handle large volumes. Today, many job ads will ask for resumes to be emailed to the company or will direct you to a website where you can file your resume electronically.

Take the time to do the research and become proficient with the development of both your cover letter and your resume. It's just another step in giving yourself an edge in the competitive world of work and is another valuable commodity that will help you get to the next step, the Interview

Interview

Most people feel some kind of anxiety when faced with meeting a stranger whose job it is to scrutinize them and determine whether they are right for the job. Keep in mind, that they want the successful applicant to be you so that their search is over and the position filled. Consider the interview a grand opportunity to 'sell' yourself. As harsh as it may sound, remember that we are all 'products' in today's competitive work-world and must market ourselves accordingly.

Think about a simple bottle of water and what points you would make to highlight the benefits of water if you were trying to sell it. You must focus on and highlight those aspects of your personality, skills, talents, and experiences that will stand out in the eyes of the interviewer.

First and foremost, you must be well-groomed and dressed appropriately, as this is the initial impression you make before you get to extol your virtues in spoken word. Remember to smile, be upbeat, and project confidence without being cocky. From the onset, be yourself... many recruiters have had training in personality types and psychology to better equip them for making decisions regarding people. They can spot a phoney. That is why it is also important not to lie. In doing so, you may be giving out signals that you are unaware of, that the interviewer will pick up on; not to mention the fact that you may regret having been untruthful down the road if you are hired. Remember to make eye contact with the person or people in the room.

Be prepared for the interview. Researching the job and company will help you be more confident going into the session and will better prepare you for any questions that might be asked of you. Successful answers will show the recruiter that you have done your research and are truly interested in the job and the organization. Don't be afraid to have to take a moment to reflect on a question if you are suddenly stumped. It is better to give the question a thorough examination instead of saying the first thing that comes to mind. You should also have prepared your own questions for the interviewer. Again, this shows your interest and will also give you further insight into the position.

Be sure to highlight your skills, talents, and anything that says to them that you are right for this job. Give personal examples from your past work and life experiences that will help reinforce these talents and skills.

Finally, if they do not offer you the information, ask if there is a time frame for making the decision and when you might hear from them. Since some employers only contact successful applicants, it is fine to make one follow-up call. But don't turn the prospective employer off by making numerous calls and badgering them. A follow up letter is also a good idea. It shows your continued interest and gives you the opportunity to give any further pertinent information you may have come up with since leaving the interview and being able to think without being under pressure. In the event that you are not hired for the position, ask for feedback as to why you weren't accepted to further assist you with your job search.

As always, explore the numerous resources available to you in helping you prepare and deal with an interview, such as the ones mentioned previously. Become a 'sponge' and take in as much information as you can!

Identifying and Dealing with Your Roadblocks

It's 'gut-check' time, folks; time to honestly explore your life and yourself! The Greek philosopher Socrates said, "Know thyself," words of wisdom to which we should all pay attention. You've probably heard it said that you can't really respect someone else or love someone else unless you respect and love yourself first. I believe this to be true. If you are having a difficult time finding employment or keeping a job, it just might be that you have issues in your life that are contributing to this dilemma.

Life is not easy. We are bombarded daily by many stressors and many of us have accumulated our share of baggage along the way. The only way you will ever be able to find success is to confront the roadblocks and conquer them. Remember, a roadblock is just that: a block. It is not a dead end. You will turn it into a dead end if you simply turn around and walk away from it. Instead, you need to thoroughly assess the block and then come up with a course of action such as climbing it, going around it, busting through it, or tearing it down altogether.

You may have a problem with your hygiene or with dressing in an inappropriate manner. You may be hindered by a lack of transportation or childcare. Perhaps you have acquired poor work habits, have a problem with authority figures, or find constant conflict with co-workers. Anger management issues may be standing in your way. Maybe you are lacking in physical capabilities, have a learning disability, or are not able to adapt to shift work. All of these factors can have a hand in making it difficult to maintain a job and must be addressed.

One of the major roadblocks you could have is substance abuse and addictions. We live in a world where it is commonplace for bargaining agreements to include the availability of rehabilitation programs for employees who suffer with substance abuse. Chances are that if you are struggling with an addiction, you are not only having a hard time progressing within your job or job search but most likely in your life as well.

The good news is that there is always hope and help available to those who want it; and that is the key. First, you have to identify the problem, sincerely admit that you have the problem, and then genuinely want to correct the problem. Of course, this is never easy but there are plenty of programs and support systems available to you. Talk to and ask for advice from family, friends (provided they are not part of the problem), co-workers, employers, religious leaders and physicians. Arm yourself with information, knowledge, support, and most of all, faith, in whatever battle you are facing!

By eliminating any roadblocks you discover you have, you automatically increase the probability of getting and maintaining a job. Until you deal with them, you are beat before you even begin. If you have already taken the steps and time to learn about and deal with questions one to four, you're headed in the right direction! I believe that then, you have it in you to be able to deal with question-five and put yourself in a position for success!

Breaking Down My Roadblocks

"To live is to suffer; to survive is to find some meaning in the suffering." Friedrich Nietzsche's words hit the mark when I consider the path I have travelled to come to this point in my life. I have certainly experienced my own fair share of difficulty and challenges in my life, but one thing I could do right and which always brought me some solace was my work. If I became addicted to anything to try and escape the rest of my life, it was work. It was the one thing I could control while other circumstances were often out of my control. Unfortunately, there was a point at which not dealing with my problems finally affected my career. I could no longer do my job effectively and to the best of my ability under those circumstances.

Thankfully, I woke up to the fact that as long as I remained the victim and focused my attention on that role, I was never going to be able to realize my true goals in life. I had to do some serious soul searching and praying. I also had to be able to forgive those in my life that had caused me pain. I discovered that holding on to anger and resentment was like 'drinking poison and expecting someone else to die.'

I finally stood face to face with the obstacle, instead of turning around and going back in the same direction from which I had come. I destroyed my roadblocks completely, and moved forward into a new area of happiness, contentment, and inner peace.

chapter 7

GOAL SETTING?

Creating an Action Plan to Realize Your Goals

"To reach a port, we must sail. Sail, not tie at anchor. Sail, not drift."

Franklin Roosevelt

We set goals on a daily basis. Half of the time you may not even be aware that you have actually set a goal, but think about it. The very act of setting an alarm clock is a step you've taken in achieving the goal of getting up in the morning at a certain hour; and that goal was to further achieve another goal, such as making it to work on time. Some people like writing to-do lists in order to get things done. They are actually writing down goals.

Setting goals affects outcomes in four ways:

1. Choice: Goals narrow attention and direct efforts to goal-relevant activities and away from perceived desirable and goal-irrelevant actions.

2. Effort: Goals can lead to more effort. In other words, one may work more intensely than one normally would to reach the goal.

3. Persistence: An individual becomes more prone to work through setbacks if pursuing a goal.

4. Cognition: Goals can lead an individual to develop cognitive strategies to change their behaviour.

Goals that are difficult to achieve and specific tend to increase performance more than goals that are not, and a goal can become more specific through quantification or enumeration. Some people set overall life goals such as whether or not they want to have a family; where they want to be financially when they retire; what kind of a lifestyle they want to live to give them a better chance of living a very long life; how they want to experience pleasure and enjoy their down time.

It is obvious that once you have made a decision on which career you intend to pursue, you have to set a goal and construct and initiate a plan for reaching that goal. Before we get into creating an action plan, however, I would like you to read the following story to reiterate the importance of setting your sight on a specific goal and working hard to achieve it.

Alfred Hitchcock, a grocer's son, got a job as a clerk when he finished school. He used his artistic talent to train as a draftsman and was launched on a promising career. Then, an American movie company; Famous Players Lasky Studios, opened an office in London. Alfred made an assortment of silent-film title cards for them, and he was thrilled when he was offered the job of studio artist.

His family felt that leaving steady, safe employment to gamble his future on something so different and new was rash and foolish, but Hitchcock understood the risks. He resolved to learn every aspect of the business. He became the studio workhorse. He helped out everywhere – with story plots, scripts, scene designing, and as assistant director.

Eight years later he got his chance to direct. His fast pace of telling a story was unique. Bold camera angles, with quick cuts and sudden close-ups, made him the master of the suspense thriller. Hitchcock's genius was immediately recognized, but from the start his greatest resource had been the determination to work harder than anybody to be the best. Every aspect of his films bore the mark of his hard-worn professionalism.

> When laying a plan to achieve your goals, keep in mind the values of hard work and persistence. They can make the difference!

Outlining and Constructing Your Plan

When you have established what your ultimate goal is, the first important thing you must do before formalizing a plan to reach that goal is to examine your commitment to the objective. How bad do you want it? Too many people have wish lists and are only fooling themselves if they are not prepared to go the distance. Remember, the path to your goal is a journey that will involve hard work, resolve, and the courage and determination to take on any obstacles you may encounter along the way. It will all pay off if you stubbornly stay the course – reach that goal and the rewards will be priceless!

Your goal is a destination you wish to reach at the end of your journey. When preparing to make a trip to a place you've never been before, it is a good idea to map out your journey. The action plan that you devise to reach your goal is like your GPS. It will help you have a clear idea of the steps you must take to get to where you want to be.

Start by writing down the goal with the day's date. It is crucial to physically write things down and record your journey rather than just developing the plan in your mind. Putting your plan on paper will give it more substance. Refer to the outline daily and even keep a diary to highlight your journey. This will keep it foremost in your mind and help you to 'keep the fire burning.' Keeping the passion and desire to attain your goal is critical.

After you have documented your long-term vision and the starting date, the next step is to set a realistic target date for completion. Is it something you can attain in a year, five years, ten or longer?

Next, do some brainstorming and consider what short-term goals you'll need as stepping stones to achieve realization of your long-term objective. Short-term goals can cover a period of weeks or months. Document them and why they are important. It is also imperative to get started immediately by considering what it is you can do right now as your first positive step towards bringing yourself closer to your goal. Why have you chosen this step and how will it help?

It is also important to consider the support you will require to take this first step and the subsequent courses of action to follow. What kind of support will you need? Where will the support come from and when? Remember to keep yourself surrounded by positive support. It can be helpful to share your intentions and dreams with others, as long as they are people who will be positive with and for you. Steer clear of any friends or family members who might have a propensity for being negative and pessimistic about your goals. You don't need people planting seeds of doubt in your mind when you have already determined that this is something you really want and know you can achieve.

The same goes for the language you use when writing your plan and documenting your journey. Keep it positive, present tense, and fun. Write a clear and concise action statement about the steps that you plan to take, in a certain order, towards your goal. Use 'I' statements for affirmation. You could start your statement off with a simple sentence demonstrating a positive view of your future. For example: "CONGRATULATIONS! Today I retire from a very enjoyable and successful career. The year is____ (your projected target date)." Brainstorm about the great things that have happened and the accomplishments you have made along the way.

When you have finalized your goal statement, write your signature at the bottom of it, treating it like a legal document. Consider it a "promissory note" to yourself and refer to it regularly as you move forward and work towards that goal.

Document compelling reasons for why you must achieve your goal. Seek out and write down a favourite inspirational quote or slogan, or a motivating and stimulating statement. There are many good sites on the Internet devoted to quotes, motivational statements, and speeches. Surround yourself with visuals that will help you better envision your goal such as pictures, photographs, drawings, or symbols. These will aid greatly in reminding you daily of your goal and in keeping it at the forefront of your life.

As well, frequently visualize what things will be like once you have reached your goal – the more you think about that end-result in your conscious mind, the more your subconscious mind will be subjected to it and act accordingly in harmony with your plan. Picture that dream home, new car, or fit body. In the case of a career goal, imagine yourself in that position and the benefits that accompany it. It may seem like day-dreaming, but in reality it is just helping you reinforce the whole process.

As always, keep in mind that journeys are usually not without challenges, obstacles, setbacks and, above all, changes. If you are forced to reconsider and revise some aspects of your plan along the way, do not consider this failure. Rather, take heart in the fact that you had the insight and were observant enough to notice that something just wasn't right and that you had to act on it in order to allow you to continue towards that ultimate goal. That, in itself, is a victory!

Finally, when that day eventually arrives and you have reached your goal, rejoice! You have every right to be proud of yourself. My guess is that you will feel much better about yourself too. Mark that date for posterity and do one last little bit of brainstorming, reflecting on the journey and how you got to your desired destination.

Don't be discouraged if it takes you longer than expected to reach your goal. Remember that the target date is not the most important thing but reaching the goal is! Writing all you can about the path you took and the circumstances along the way will help you in setting and reaching other future goals. Don't forget to document any obstacles you faced along the way and how you successfully dealt with them; "That which does not kill us, makes us stronger!"

Have courage and don't be afraid to aim high when setting goals. If you really want it and are prepared to work hard and even make sacrifices, you can have it. Vince Lombardi, the legendary professional football coach, for whom the Super Bowl trophy is named, is famous for saying, "The dictionary is the only place that success comes before work; hard work is the price we must pay for success. I think you can accomplish anything if you're willing to pay the price."

One final thought before I share a story with you and send you on your way to begin your wonderful journey of seeking out and discovering your dream career. Have you ever known anyone who constantly spouted off about what great things they planned on accomplishing or attaining? You know the people I'm talking about. Every time you run into them the story's the same, but their situation hasn't changed one bit. They can 'talk the talk' but aren't 'walking the walk.' They fool themselves and try to fool others with their grandiose pipedreams. Don't be one of those people. Put an end to pretending and make that honest effort to become a better person with a better life.

A Funny Thing Happened on the Way to Kitchener

Recently, a friend called me and invited me on a trip that sounded quite fascinating and I was excited about the opportunity. I was going to travel to Kitchener (for those of you unfamiliar, it is a city in southern Ontario, west of Toronto, Canada) to see the long-time Canadian rocker, Kim Mitchell in concert. What made it all the more interesting was the fact that I had never seen him perform before, and even better was the fact that one of the persons accompanying us on the trip was the father of one of Kim's guitar players. There seemed to be a good chance that I was going to be able to experience behind-the-scenes and meet Kim Mitchell and his band after the show.

The journey started out normal and pleasant enough. We had less than a two-hour journey ahead of us and left that day around 5:30 p.m. It was Thanksgiving weekend and the annual Oktoberfest celebration was taking place in Kitchener with the concert slated to start at 8:30 p.m. My friend drove and was joined by her uncle, who sat up front with her while I shared the back with my friend's friend, the guitar player's father.

As we headed out, my friend assured all of us that she knew where she was going. Unfortunately, nothing could have been further from the truth and what I had envisioned as being a fun evening would turn out to be a nightmare. After driving for a little while we made a quick stop at a Tim Horton's. When we got back on the road, the chaos slowly started. It appeared that my friend wasn't as sure of her directions as she had led us to believe and, to make matters worse, her uncle, who was a bit of a character, decided to tease her by pushing a bunch of different buttons in her car. You could say that he was literally 'pushing her buttons!'

Now the car's four-way lights were flashing and my friend apparently didn't know how to shut them off and she was yelling at her uncle; and somewhere along the way we missed a turn or something, because and after driving for some time it became obvious that we were lost. Now the rest of us started to offer our advice, but my friend was just freaking out, which only led to more chaos. While I was instructing my friend that we were supposed to be on a certain highway, the tension increased, and in her attempt to pull over and correct the flashing light problem, we were almost involved in what would have surely been a very serious accident.

Eventually the guitar player's father reached his son on his cell phone and got proper directions from him. His son told him that we were about forty-five minutes away. The time was now 7:30 p.m. We finally reached the city of Kitchener but were not sure where the arena was at which the concert was being held. We must have asked ten different people for directions, but for some odd reason my friend kept driving away before the directions were complete. Now I was thinking, this was ridiculous and I happened to mutter something along the lines of, "We'll be lucky to make it for the encore," which just further infuriated my friend.

Believe me, if I had reached the point where had I had the finances and the opportunity, I would have called a cab and headed back home. Eventually, I calmed down, having decided that I couldn't really control the situation I was in anyway. I was even able to find some purpose in the whole episode when I realized that God was allowing this to happen to give me a good example-story to share with all of you. I believe that everything happens for a reason and you have to try and find the positives in all situations.

Finally, we found an arena, but of course, it wasn't the correct arena, and it was 8:45. We were told that the arena we wanted was on the other side of town and fifteen minutes away. By the time we got near our destination, the father had received a call from his son wondering where we were because they had already finished the show and were off the stage. The night was officially a bust.

So we started our journey back home. Since it had been a while since we had been out of the van, another stop at a Timmy's was in order. At this time we secured proper directions to get back to the Niagara area and rolled into town around 12:45 in the morning. Not only had I missed out on the concert (and Oktoberfest, for that matter), but I had just spent the best part of the evening in a van, except for the two donut shop stops; and I was scheduled to make a Thanksgiving brunch for my family later that morning.

I wasn't too pleased at the time but when I look back now it all seems so humorous and it does make me chuckle. My whole point for sharing this story with you is this: You can travel for a long time and a good many miles, but it doesn't guarantee that you will get to where you want to be. The same is true for pursuing your dreams and goals. If you don't have a well-thought out plan and solid directions for your journey, you are sure to get lost along the way.

I would like to leave you with a few inspirational quotes...something to keep close to your heart and mind. God bless you all!

> "He who fails to plan, plans to fail."
> "Failure is success if we learn from it."
>
> Malcolm Forbes

> "Success is going from failure to failure without loss of enthusiasm."
>
> Winston Churchill

> "Success is getting up more times than you fall down."
>
> Forest Fisher

Revelations from a Co-Author, Silent until Now

I hope that you have been helped and inspired by this book. Ironically, I don't think I can properly express in words just what an impact being its ghost-writer has had on me, but I will try. Denise brought this project to me at a time when I had just become unemployed myself. I can't say that the job I'd lost was my dream job, but it was work that I usually enjoyed, it paid the bills, and I had done it for the past twelve years; a record when it comes to my employment history.

I had been working for a small demolition company that a friend had started up. Eventually, I ended up renting a room at my boss's house and times were good; I had a nice roof over my head and fairly steady employment...for a few years. Work suddenly slowed down and my friend experienced financial difficulties and ultimately lost his house, which also put his business in limbo. Suddenly I was not only out of a job but I was homeless as well. My financial situation was not much better and I was in no position to get a place of my own at that time, so my son was gracious enough to rescue me and take me in.

This dramatic and traumatic change in my life, however, was about to open up a window of opportunity. Staying with my son brought me in regular contact with his mother, since we share a two and half-year-old grandson and she would come for weekly visits to see the little guy when he was over for the weekend.

If you haven't already guessed it by now, the woman I'm speaking of is Denise Conway, the visionary behind this book, and my first wife and mother of our son Ryan and his beautiful sister Stesha. Now, after our period of estrangement, Denise and I were working together on her dream project, and it was like my life had come full circle

Denise's plans for the book had started several years before she came to me but as she mentions in the book, her strength is more in speaking than it is in writing, and she was having difficulty making the book a reality.

During our earlier relationship so many years before, she had discovered that I had a talent for writing. I used to write her poems and songs and had always done well in school, especially with regards to English and Composition. Denise is a very smart woman! Not only did she know that commissioning me to write this book would help her realize a dream, but she was also aware of the profound and positive influence it would have on me at a time when I really needed it. Suddenly I had purpose in my life again and I was learning so much about this new subject; one that I could certainly relate to, having been on and off the 'job rollercoaster' my entire life. To give you an idea of that history, I have been a security guard, a member of the police force, a vacuum cleaner salesman, an ambulance attendant, a delivery driver for a trucking repair firm, a bartender (more than a couple of times), a roofer, a landscaper, a mover (both household and commercial), a professional musician, a registered practical nurse and, of course, a demolition-construction labourer. And I know I haven't listed all of the jobs. Not the most stable employment history, to say the least. But now, thanks to Denise's insight and inspiration, I have a better understanding of myself and my gifts and skills and realize that writing is what I should be doing. I hope you get the opportunity some day to hear her speak. She has a dynamic personality, an infectious laugh, is as beautiful on the inside as she is on the outside, and truly cares about people and wants to help them succeed as she has succeeded.

I consider myself blessed to have met her and for the role she has played in my life. She has inspired me to look at the positives in life. Our union, although it didn't last, still produced a wonderful son and eventually, an adorable grandson, Aidan. Denise has conquered the demons in her past and has helped me conquer a few of my own. I believe that God has a reason for everything, including this book.

My prayer for all of you is that our book will enlighten you and help you discover your gifts and talents, the 'real you,' and that you will use this to create a game-winning plan for achievement. I could say 'good luck' with your career search, but luck has nothing to do with it. Equip yourself with knowledge, a positive attitude, and a passionate desire to put forth a sincere effort, and I am certain that you will one day realize the career of your dreams!

May God bless you!
D.G. MacPherson

The Final Word

The only way that I have survived this journey is to know that God had a plan for all of it…the good, the bad and the ugly. As long as I trusted him and loved him, he would be faithful to me. He definitely turned this mess into a masterpiece. I wake up every morning wondering what great things God has planned for me today.

My spiritual journey began ten years ago at a very low point in my life. I was flipping through the channels and saw Joyce Myers, and the words I remembered her saying were, "Do you want to meet a man that won't rape, beat, or abuse you? His name is Jesus!" For several years I had shut myself in and spent a lot of time reflecting on my life and asking God to heal what was broken.

He is true to his word and I wouldn't change the journey because it has made me who I am today and I am exactly who God created me to be.

With God, ANYTHING is possible!
Denise Conway

AKNOWLEDGEMENTS

First and foremost, I would like to thank God for turning my pain into purpose so that I am able to help others find their career paths, happiness, and peace.

Thank you to my children, Ryan and Stesha, for loving and supporting me in the most difficult of times. They believed in me even when I didn't believe in myself. When the world disappointed me, they were always there to help me get back up one more time.

I am very grateful to my ex-mother-in-law Ruby Conway. God rest her soul. A few months prior to her death, she suggested to me that I should write a book and entitle it, "The Queen of Hearts." I was very touched that she saw me in that light and I am considering writing that book next. During one of our visits, she imparted these very wise words to me: "Denise, make a little noise so the world will know that you were here." I know that she is smiling down on me.

I am so grateful for a chance encounter several years ago that introduced me to Joseph Sherren. He has inspired me and is an amazing role model. Thanks so much, Joe. You're the best and the real deal! A true gift from heaven.

A big thank you goes out to my close friends; Elaine, Louella, Jim, Wendy, Patty, Trudy, Christine, Nicole, Caroline, Carole, Trevor and Sherri who all had such positive impacts on my life. They helped me in so many ways when I couldn't help myself anymore. They loved me and that is the best medicine of all!

I would like to extend my thanks and gratitude to all of the spiritual and inspirational mentors who have imparted the most valuable life lessons to me. They include Paster Sam Jeeva, Joyce Myers, James and

Betty Robinson, Beth Moore, Creflo Dollar, Benny Hinn, Tina and Ian at Victory Church, Canadian edition.

Finally, I would like to express my sincere thanks to all of the clients I have had the pleasure of working with throughout my career. Your desire and interest in making better lives for yourselves and the stories you have shared with me have inspired me and have brought me much pleasure and satisfaction throughout my career as an employment counsellor.

CPSIA information can be obtained at www.ICGtesting.com
Printed in the USA
BVOW06s1918110216

436422BV00003B/4/P